OLIVER CROMWELL
and his world

A reconstruction of Oliver Cromwell's coat of arms over the doorway of Cromwell House, Huntingdon, which is on the site of the house where he was born in 1599

IT COULD ONLY HAVE HAPPENED in an age of revolutionary storms such as shook almost the whole of Europe in the mid-seventeenth century. But even then it was a sensation that a modest English country gentleman should be able to push through the trial and execution of his King and later himself become Lord Protector of the united Commonwealth of England, Scotland and Ireland. That is what Oliver Cromwell achieved in the space of just over ten years before he died, worn out, at the age of fifty-nine.

The Cromwells had been one of the two most prosperous and politically influential families in Huntingdonshire in eastern England ever since the Protestant Reformation. The county was not one of the richest in the kingdom; in the winter, and sometimes in the summer too, the rivers burst their banks and the population, who scraped a living from the fenlands lying between the university town of Cambridge and the borough of Huntingdon, had to go about their business on stilts. But the Cromwells owned much workable farming land in the county and elsewhere in East Anglia; both of Oliver's grandfathers had profited substantially from the dissolution of the monasteries by Henry VIII. Oliver's wealthy uncle, after whom he was named, frequently acted as host to James I at his palatial mansion of Hinchingbrooke just outside Huntingdon, as his own father had earlier entertained Elizabeth I there.

Oliver's father, a conscientious landlord and justice of the peace in Huntingdon, inherited only the portion of a second son, and his wife, Elizabeth (born Steward), who came from Norfolk, brought him quite a small dowry. In modern terms their annual income might have been in the £4,000 to £5,000 range. They formed a prolific clan. One of Cromwell's paternal aunts gave birth to Edward Whalley, who was to serve him as a major-general; another was the mother of John Hampden, who was to be a fellow member of parliament with Oliver in the House of Commons. Oliver's only maternal uncle, Thomas Steward of Ely, was to leave his nephew valuable property and enable him to surmount the financial difficulties under which he laboured in the first years of his married life.

Elizabeth Cromwell, Oliver's mother (born Steward): painting by an unknown artist now at Chequers

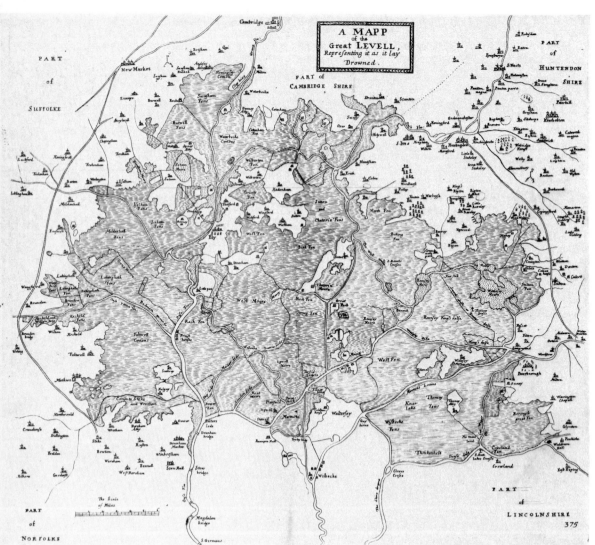

(*Above left*) a seventeenth-century engraving of Cambridge from the west

(*Above*) a general view of the country around Cambridge almost as it must have been in Cromwell's day. Oliver became a member of parliament for Cambridge in 1640

(*Opposite*) a map of the Great Level in east England representing it as 'drowned'. During the seventeenth century Dutch methods were first introduced to drain the fenlands, which included extensive areas of Cambridgeshire and Huntingdonshire

A caricature of Dr Thomas Beard, who was Oliver Cromwell's schoolmaster and friend

Oliver himself was the fifth child of his parents (he was born on 25 April 1599), who had ten children altogether. His two brothers died young; his father died when Oliver was eighteen. So he was the only man in a family of women before he himself married and in his turn fathered five sons and four daughters.

Oliver received his education in the local grammar school at Huntingdon where his master, Dr Thomas Beard, a friend of the family, was a strict and combative Puritan who later became vicar of one of the four churches in the town. Then Oliver went to Sidney Sussex College, Cambridge, a new foundation that won a reputation as a nursery of Puritans, the head of the College being a deeply introspective Calvinist. Oliver left Cambridge after his father's death in 1617 and returned home to attend to family affairs. Later, according to his earliest biographers, he studied law in Lincoln's Inn before in 1620 he married Elizabeth Bourchier, the daughter of a City of London merchant. It is unlikely that it was a love match. This pattern – education at the local grammar school, a pleasant year or two in

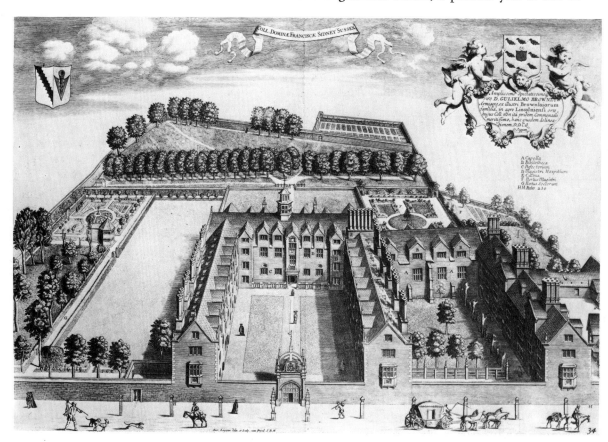

Sidney Sussex College, Cambridge, where Oliver was a fellow-commoner for about a year (1616–17)

Cambridge as a privileged fellow-commoner, a year or two at one of the London Inns of Court and an early arranged marriage – was typical of the youthful life of English country gentlemen in Oliver's day and age.

In the course of his upbringing Oliver learned enough Latin to be able to speak it (it was the diplomatic language), and some elementary mathematics. Under the impulse of his teachers and parents he read the Bible from cover to cover and learned by heart passages from the Old Testament, particularly the Psalms. But nothing in contemporary tradition suggests that Oliver was exceptionally studious. His tutor at Cambridge was said to have observed that he 'was not so much addicted to speculation as to action'; one of the physicians who attended him when he was Lord Protector wrote that 'he laid an unsolid foundation of learning at Cambridge, but was soon cloy'd with studies, delighting more in horses and pastimes abroad in the fields.' That is likely enough. Farming and hunting were the normal occupations of country gentlemen and they rarely left their homes except to attend the quarter sessions as unpaid magistrates or to visit London when the House of Commons was sitting, if they were elected members.

In the time between his marriage and his election as one of the two members for Huntingdon early in 1628, Oliver passed through a searing psychological experience which affected his body as well as his mind. He had been left an orphan; two-thirds of his small patrimony was assigned by his father to maintain the widowed mother and her daughters; his uncle, Sir Oliver, ruined by extravagance, was forced to sell up at Hinchingbrooke to meet the demands of money-lenders; Oliver himself failed to make arable farming pay in Huntingdon and in 1631 moved to St Ives to become a grazier; and, stimulated by his Bible reading, he underwent the spiritual agony known as 'conversion' from which he emerged convinced that he was now one of God's Chosen People or Elect accepted 'in His Son' and enabled 'to walk in the light'.

Dr John Symcotts, the physician who looked after the Cromwells and other leading gentry in East Anglia (the poor could not afford a doctor), is reputed to have said that Oliver sometimes sent for him in the middle of the night because he believed that he was dying. Symcotts recorded in his case-book that Oliver took a universal cure-all 'to avoid the plague' but only 'found it effective against pimples'. Sir Theodore Mayerne, the King's doctor and probably the greatest physician of his time, noted in his case-book in September 1628 that Cromwell was 'exceedingly melancholy'. Another of the King's doctors, writing admittedly in the reign of Charles II, asserted that Oliver had been a hypochondriac for thirty years. Most of these stories appear to relate to the period around 1628 before Cromwell was first elected a member of parliament.

Elizabeth (born Bourchier), whom Oliver Cromwell married on 22 August 1620

(*Right*) Westminster as it was in the Cromwellian period

(*Below*) Cromwell House, Ely: a nineteenth-century watercolour; and (*far right*) a photograph of the house as it looks today. Cromwell moved to Ely from St Ives in 1638 to a property which he inherited from his maternal uncle, Thomas Steward, who had been reasonably well-to-do

In that House of Commons Oliver showed himself to be a violent Puritan attacking the 'tyranny' of Charles I's High Church bishops. He was doing what he could to promote preaching instead of the reading of homilies which was the practice of many Church of England clergy. For all kinds of Puritans – and there were many small sects – believed in the value of preaching and extemporary prayer rather than the use of ritual and strict adherence to the Book of Common Prayer. So it is reasonable to assume that Oliver was 'converted' about this date and was ready to proclaim his religious beliefs. After that his troubles began to clear up. Although he was to bury his eldest son, Robert, when he was eighteen, Oliver had three others who grew to manhood and four daughters, three of whom survived him. In 1638 Oliver received his expected inheritance from his maternal uncle and settled in Ely, where he became one of the leading citizens and concerned himself with local questions.

After Charles I had dissolved his third parliament in 1629, because its members criticized his religious policy and what they considered to be arbitrary taxation, he did not call another for eleven years. Many country gentlemen and former members of parliament like Oliver grew discontented over the government's handling of affairs in both Church and State. Tradition has it that Oliver was so disgusted that he contemplated selling his newly acquired property in Ely and emigrating to New England. The celebrated parliamentary leader, John Pym, also thought of emigrating at the same time. But most of the emigrants were less prominent men and were attracted to America by the hope of acquiring cheap land as much as freedom from religious persecution. Even Oliver's future friends, Harry Vane and Hugh Peter, who both went for a time to New England, soon returned. Their aim was to put matters right at home, not to abandon the kingdom to what they regarded as tyranny.

John Pym, an acknowledged leader in the House of Commons when it met in 1640

Oliver Cromwell, like many other radical Christians of his time, wanted to purify the Church of England, not to separate himself from it. It was only during the period of William Laud's supremacy – he became Archbishop of Canterbury in 1633 – that Oliver twice thought of closing down his East Anglian home and sailing away with his family to America. For after his conversion he felt sure that the Holy Spirit had entered his soul and thus directed his actions. 'The best of us,' he was to say, 'are, God knows, poor weak saints; yet saints; if not sheep, yet lambs; and must be fed.' Many of the radical clergy who were to serve in the Parliamentarian armies as chaplains inculcated the doctrine of the Holy Spirit, putting faith before works; for they were convinced that the moral law did not bind Christians who were under the law of Free Grace. Dr John Owen, a prolific theologian, whom Cromwell was to appoint Vice-Chancellor of Oxford University in 1652, was a pioneer of the doctrine that personal experience, that is to say 'conversion', afforded proof of the indwelling of the Holy Spirit. Government by the Holy Spirit enabled the individual to measure 'the glorious dispensations of God'. Hence the views of clergy whom Cromwell admired, men like Owen, Peter Sterry, John Saltmarsh, William Dell, John and Thomas Goodwin and Philip Nye, were above all individualist (or 'sectarian') and Congregationalist. They believed that, with the aid of the Holy Spirit, they could interpret the Bible for themselves, though they were not bound by any laws. But even the Bible need not be the final guide; for, said Oliver, God 'speaks without a written word sometimes, yet according to it.' It was not a quietist creed; men had to show forth their faith by their lives. The significance of belief must issue in action and conduct. Thus, wrote Joshua Sprigge, another of the army chaplains, 'men conquer better as they are Saints than Soldiers.'

(*Right*) William Laud: a portrait dated 1635. Laud was the leader of the High Church or 'Arminian' party. He had been appointed Bishop of London in 1630 and Archbishop of Canterbury in 1633. The cartoon (*above*) shows Laud dining on the ears of William Prynne, John Bastwick and Henry Burton. These three were Puritans who were condemned by the Court of Star Chamber, of which Laud was a member, for seditious libel in 1637

After his conversion Oliver won a local reputation as a strong individualist who was ready to defy authority, whether it was that of High Churchmen, such as Matthew Wren, the Bishop of Ely, the borough council in Huntingdon or the capitalists who were aiming to obtain money out of draining the Cambridgeshire soil to the detriment of the poverty-stricken fenmen. Oliver became known as a benevolent 'Lord of the Fens'. Because of that, the former member for Huntingdon was chosen to be one of the two members of parliament for Cambridge after he had been sworn a freeman of the town on the payment of one penny to the poor.

Thus Oliver was amongst those who sat in the House of Commons, listening on 17 April 1640 to a vigorous speech by the veteran politician, John Pym, in which he outlined three sets of grievance felt by the country gentry against the government of Charles I: grievances 'against the liberties and privileges of parliament'; grievances against 'innovations in matters of religion'; and grievances over property rights. Comprehended in the latter were various devices

13

that had been employed by the Crown to raise money during the eleven years when no parliament sat, such as the levying of 'ship money' on inland towns and the exaction of fines from gentlemen who refused to accept knighthoods. Oliver evidently paid both these charges, but his cousin, John Hampden, had brought a test case against the Crown on the levying of ship money, which he lost. The King now offered to abandon ship money in return for a generous financial supply voted by the Commons. He needed this largely because he had been unsuccessfully waging war on his Scottish subjects who objected to the imposition upon them of a prayer book modelled on Anglican lines. When financial aid was refused, Charles dissolved this Short Parliament.

John Pym was not a conscious revolutionary, but he was an out-spoken critic of what he believed to be arbitrary government and he was no friend to the bishops. After the Short Parliament had broken up, meetings were held to discuss unresolved grievances raised there, meetings which were attended by men ranging from aristocrats like

Broughton Castle, Oxford, a house belonging to William Fiennes, Lord Saye and Sele, where Cromwell's friends met to discuss political tactics. Saye and Sele was a friend and business associate of Pym and a critic of the King's Government in the House of Commons

the third Earl of Essex and Lord Saye and Sele to young Harry Vane, who had been elected for Hull, Oliver St John, a rising London barrister who had represented John Hampden in the ship-money case, and John Hampden himself. The meetings took place in Lord Saye's country house, at Pym's house in London and in the home of Hampden's son-in-law in Northamptonshire. Undoubtedly Hampden's cousin, the fiery member for Cambridge, was invited to such meetings. A policy was worked out which would compel the King to assuage their grievances.

So when Charles I, once more defeated in Scotland and still in desperate need of money, summoned a fresh parliament in the autumn of 1640, Oliver Cromwell, again elected for Cambridge, became, under the leadership of 'King Pym', one of the most indignant critics of the government. He sat on many committees and took part in many debates. He expressed his resentment at 'popish innovations' which were being forced on Cambridge and his anger over the activities of the Bishop of Ely; and he was appointed a member of a committee to consider complaints against him. Oliver even went so far as to advocate the abolition of all archbishops and bishops and the whole hierarchy of the existing Church 'root and branch'; if that could not be accepted he wanted to exclude the bishops from the House of Lords and confine them to purely spiritual functions. To increase the power of parliament he urged the King to agree to a Bill stipulating that parliament should meet every year or, failing that, every three years.

(*Left*) Henry Vane the Younger, at one time an intimate friend of Oliver Cromwell but he broke with Cromwell during the Protectorate

(*Right*) John Hampden, another close friend of Oliver Cromwell, with whom he discussed the training of the Parliamentarian army. He was famous for having refused to pay ship money to the Crown. Hampden was killed in the early stages of the first civil war

But Pym's approach to the problem of subjecting the monarchy to the wishes of the majority in Parliament was more direct and more ruthless than Cromwell's. He was content to lay on one side the question of abolishing the bishops, though in May 1641 he voted for a Bill, sponsored by Oliver Cromwell and Harry Vane, to do it. Instead Pym concentrated on attacking the King's 'evil counsellors', headed by Thomas Wentworth, Earl of Strafford and Lord Lieutenant of Ireland, who was accused of treason principally on the ground that he had advised Charles I to bring over an army from Ireland to coerce his English subjects. Another minister of the Crown, Lord Finch, who had defended the levying of ship money, was also accused of treason; so was Secretary of State Windebank, who was charged with granting favours to Roman Catholics. The last two managed to flee abroad from the wrath of the Commons. But neither William Laud, Archbishop of Canterbury, nor Bishop Wren escaped the enmity of Pym. The Archbishop was accused of supporting Strafford and sustaining Wren and 'all the other wicked bishops now in England'.

Once Charles had weakly yielded to the demand by parliament that he should allow Strafford to be put to death and that Laud should be kept in prison, he was compelled to give way all along the line. There is no evidence that Oliver took any part in the attack on Strafford, though he must certainly have approved of the imprisonment

The execution of Thomas Wentworth, first Earl of Strafford, on 12 May 1641. It is not known whether Oliver Cromwell played any part in the prosecution of Strafford

of Laud. But he was disappointed that his 'root-and-branch' Bill was shelved and that the Book of Common Prayer was not condemned. He was actually reproved for using unparliamentary language during a debate on the abolition of the bishops. Oliver seems to have been less excited over the violation of property rights, for which the royal ministers were largely condemned, than he was over the need to purify the Church by getting rid of the bishops. For he felt deeply, as did his friends, the Congregational ministers and Puritan lecturers, that the only true 'succession' in the ministry was 'through the Spirit given in its measure'.

When Oliver returned from Ely to Westminster in the autumn of 1641 to attend the second session of what was to be known as the Long Parliament, he was still obsessed with the importance of reforming the Church. While he continued his campaign against the bishops and pressed for the abolition of the prayer book, he also advocated the delivery of sermons in all the parishes of England in the afternoon of the Sabbath. He took part in the general distrust of the King and the

An engraving of the House of Commons as it was about 1641. Oliver was then an active member who took part in the movement against the King's Government and the preparations for civil war

> 1 You ar to accuse those ~~& joyntlie~~ joyntlie & severallie
> 2 you ar to referve the power of making additionally
> 3 When the Comitie for examination is a naming (wch you must prefs to be close & under tey of fecresie) if eather Effex, Warwick, Holland, Say, ~~████~~ Wharton, or Brooke be named, you must defyre that they may be spared because you ar to examine them as witnesses for me

(Opposite) 'A Map of the Kingdom of Ireland with particular notes distinguishing the towns revolted, taken or burnt since the late Rebellion': another piece of Puritan propaganda, published as a broadsheet about 1642

King Charles I's order for the arrest of five members of the House of Commons at the end of 1641. Cromwell was not one of them, but his friends Pym and Hampden were

An Exact and true Relation
of the late Plots which were contrived and hatched in Ireland.

1. A Coppy of a Letter fent from the Lord chiefe Iuftices and Privy Councel in *Ireland*, to our parliament here in *England*.
2. Their laft Proclamation which they publifhed concerning thofe Traytors.
3. The whole Difcourfe of the Plot revealed by *Owen Ockanellee* who is now in *England*.
4. The dangerous and extraordinary deliverance of the party who narrowly efcaped with his life.
5. The reward the Parliament hath confirmed upon him.
6. The true Relation of the whole Treafon related by the Lord Keeper, to the Honourable Houfe of Commons the firft of *November*. 1641.

London Printed for *Francis Coules*. 1641.

(Above) title-page of *An Exact and True Relation of the Late Plots which were contrived and hatched in Ireland* (1641). The stories about the rising and the massacres of English Protestants in Ireland in 1641 were grossly exaggerated by the Puritans

fear that Charles intended to re-establish 'popery' and destroy Puritanism. Charles had in fact, during the recess, gone to Scotland to try to rally a Royalist party there and Pym had sent a parliamentary commission after him to spy on what he was doing. But what most perturbed the House of Commons when it reassembled was the news received from Ireland that a 'papist' rebellion had broken out there and that many Protestants were being murdered. Cromwell and his friends were unwilling to allow the King to raise a new army to suppress this rebellion (the army he had used against the Scots had been disbanded) and also demanded that he should henceforward employ only counsellors and officials whom parliament could trust. Oliver himself moved on 6 November that the Earl of Essex, who was friendly to the Puritans, should be put in command of the trained bands, that is to say the militia which was the only armed force in existence in the country. He was also working to win parliamentary control over any army that might be recruited and sent to Ireland. When that same November John Pym introduced into the Commons a Grand Remonstrance detailing the royal government's errors and requiring control over the King's ministers, Oliver spoke in its favour and was one of the narrow majority that voted for it.

Charles was provoked beyond endurance. He denied that he had any evil counsellors; he refused to admit that the Church of England needed drastic reformation; he was not going to have his officials named for him; and he was determined not to renounce the power of the sword by conceding to parliament the organization of any army to be sent to Ireland or the command over the home militia. Therefore he rejected the Grand Remonstrance and attempted to arrest Pym and four other leading members of the Commons as well as Lord Kimbolton, son of the first Earl of Manchester, a neighbour of Cromwell in East Anglia, on the ground that they had all committed treason. The attempt failed abysmally and Charles left London for the north of England not to return until, seven years later, he was put on trial for his life.

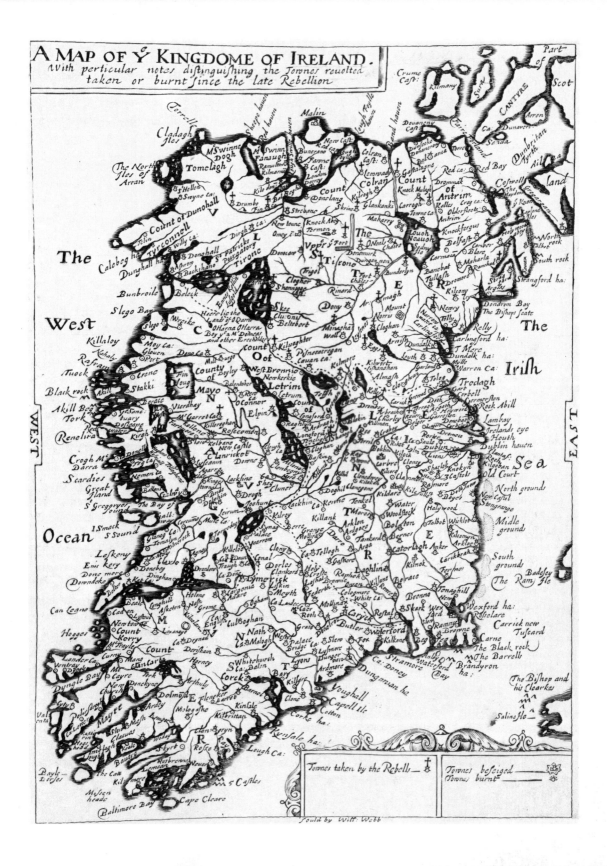

A MAP OF Yͤ KINGDOME OF IRELAND.

With perticular notes distinguishing the Townes reuolted
taken or burnt since the late Rebellion

Townes taken by the Rebells	✝	Townes besieged	
		Townes burnt	

Sould by Will: Webb

It was now becoming obvious that a real danger of civil war existed, for negotiations between the King and his parliament led nowhere. The majority of the House of Commons was diametrically opposed to the King's views on religious organization; these members demanded larger control over executive affairs, including the choice of ministers, and they fundamentally distrusted the King's policies for which they were expected to find the money.

Neither Charles nor 'King Pym' had an army, though the City of London, which possessed a proficient militia, gave its support to the Commons and frustrated the arrest of the six members. Oliver was now forty-three and in the prime of his life. To judge from the portraits by Robert Walker he had a serious and also perhaps a fanatical look about him. Now he discovered his natural element. Gradually he laid aside his preoccupation with the Church and revealed himself to be a man of action. While Pym continued to negotiate with Charles on the basis of the establishment of a constitutional monarchy, subject to parliamentary control, Oliver demanded the setting up of a committee to put the kingdom in a state of defence. He also pressed for military intervention in Ireland and subscribed handsomely to a war loan. During the summer he became a member of a committee to prevent the King from raising an army in Yorkshire and of another committee to obstruct the landing of munitions for the King's use from abroad. Finally he obtained the agreement of the Commons (from which all the Royalist sympathizers had fled) to his raising volunteers in his own constituency of Cambridge. Early in August he himself rode back to Cambridge with the aim of preventing the university from sending college plate to be melted down for the royal treasury. In this he was largely successful. A fortnight later Charles I, having rejected the parliament's peace terms, raised his standard at Nottingham and on 22 August 1642 the first English civil war began.

King Charles I and Sir Edward Walker, his Secretary-at-War, reputedly in the grounds of Nottingham Castle

(*Opposite*) Oliver Cromwell: one of the numerous portraits by Robert Walker. Walker painted Cromwell from life, but it is not known which was the original portrait

England at the time of the Civil War. Names underlined indicate battles and the dotted line shows the extent of the Eastern Association: Essex, Suffolk, Norfolk, Cambridge

Perth
• Stirling
• Leith • Dunbar
Edinburgh
• Berwick

SCOTLAND

Carlisle Newcastle

Marston Moor • York
Preston • Leeds • Hull
• Pontefract
• Warrington • Gainsborough
• Chester Lincoln• • Winceby
• Nantwich • Newark
• Nottingham
Shrewsbury • Leicester
• Ely
WALES • Naseby • Newmarket
Huntingdon • Cambridge
• Worcester • Saffron Walden
Edgehill
×
Gloucester • Oxford
Milford Haven Windsor • London
Pembroke • Reading
• Devizes Newbury • Maidstone
• Langport • Salisbury
Exeter• • Newport
Lostwithiel Carisbrooke ISLE OF WIGHT
Plymouth

The Prospect of Nottingham from Darby Roade on the West side of the Towne

Rich. Hall. delin.

Throughout the summer, although political negotiations had not been abandoned, each side eagerly recruited and collected arms. Cromwell, after seizing the castle at Cambridge, hurried back to London, but soon returned to Huntingdon to enlist a troop of light cavalry. All Cromwell's friends and relations (except his elderly uncle, Sir Oliver) were preparing for war. The quartermaster in Oliver's troop was his brother-in-law, John Desborough. Another brother-in-law, Valentine Walton, raised his own troop of horse. Oliver's eldest surviving son, a boy of nineteen, named after him, became an officer in yet another troop of horse. His cousin, John Hampden, was appointed a colonel. The Earl of Essex, whose claims to be commander Oliver himself had urged, was put in charge of the Parliamentarian army. Marching across England from East Anglia to Worcestershire, Oliver's troop joined with John Hampden's brigade and took part in the last stages of the first battle of the civil war, fought at Edgehill. Though the battle was a drawn one, Oliver was disappointed with what he saw there and pressed upon Hampden the importance of enlisting 'men of a spirit' for the Parliamentarian cavalry.

At the end of the first campaign, during which the Royalists vainly attacked London and then took up their headquarters at Oxford, Oliver returned to his constituency of Cambridge and his birthplace of Huntingdon with the aim of recruiting better cavalrymen. Promoted colonel, by the end of the year he had enlisted and trained a double cavalry regiment; amongst his officers, besides Desborough,

A contemporary view of Nottingham, where Charles I raised the standard for war in August 1642

A crown minted during the siege of Oxford, which constituted the Royalist headquarters

a Solemn LEAGUE AND COVENANT,

for Reformation, and defence of Religion, the Honour and happinesse of the king, and the Peace and safety, of the three Kingdoms of ENGLAND, SCOTLAND, and IRELAND.

Ieremia 50. 5. Come let us joyn our selves to the Lord

16 43

in a perpetuall Covenant that shall not be forgotten.

We Noblemen, Barons, Knights, Gentlemen, Citizens, Burgesses, Ministers of the Gospel, and Commons of all sorts in the kingdoms of England, Scotland, and Ireland, by the Providence of God, living under one King, and being of one reformed Religion, having before our eye the Glory of God, and the advancement of the kingdome of our Lord and Saviour Iesus Christ, the Honour and happinesse of the kings Maiesty and his posterity, and the true publique Liberty, Safety, and Peace of the Kingdoms, wherein every ones private Condition is included, and calling to minde the treacherous and bloody Plots, Conspiracies, Attempts, and Practices of the Enemies of God, against the true Religion, and professors thereof in all places, especially in these three kingdoms ever since the Reformation of Religion, and how much their rage, power and presumption, are of late, and at this time increased and exercised, whereof the deplorable state of the Church and kingdom of Ireland, the distressed estate of the Church and kingdom of England, and the dangerous estate of the Church and kingdom of Scotland, are present and publique Testimonies: We have now at last, (after other meanes of Supplication, Remonstrance, Protestations, and Sufferings) for the preservation of our selves and our Religion, from utter Ruine and Destruction; according to the commendable practice of these Kingdoms in former times, and the Example of Gods people in other Nations; After mature deliberation, resolved and determined to enter into a mutuall and solemn League and Covenant, Wherein we all subscribe, and each one of us for himself, with our hands lifted up to the most high God, do sweare;

I. That we shall sincerely, really and constantly, through the Grace of God, endeavour in our severall places and callings, the preservation of the Reformed Religion in the Church of Scotland, in Doctrine, Worship, Discipline & Government, against our common Enemies, the reformation of Religion in the kingdoms of England and Ireland, in Doctrine, Worship, Discipline and Government, according to the Word of God, and the Example of the best Reformed Churches, And shall indeavour to bring the Churches of God in the three kingdoms, to the neerest coniunction and Uniformity in Religion, Confession of Faith, Form of Church government, Directory for Worship and Catechising: That we and our posterity after us, may as Brethren, live in Faith and Love, and the Lord may delight to dwell in the midest of us.

Thou hast avouched y Lorde this day to be thy God and to walke in his wayes, & to keepe his Statutes & his Commandments & his Iudgements & to hearken to his voyce. And the Lord hath avouched thee this day to be his peculiar people & to make thee high above all nations, in prayse & name & in honour.
Deutero: 26: 17: 18:

II. That we shall in like manner, without respect of persons, indeavour the extirpation of Popery, Prelacie, (that is Church government by Arch-Bishops, Bishops, their Chancellor and Commissaries, Deans, Deans and Chapters, Archdeacons, & all other Ecclesiasticall Officers depending on that Hierarchy) Superstition, Heresie, Schisme, Prophanenesse, and whatsoever shall be found to be contrary to sound Doctrine, and the power of Godlinesse: lest we partake in other mens sins, and therby be in danger to receive of their plagues, and that the Lord may be one, and his Name one in the three kingdoms.

Every plant which my heavenly Father hath not planted shall be rooted out. Math. 15.

Corifters   *Singers*   *Deane*   *Deane*

III. We shall with the same sincerity, reality and constancy, in our severall Vocations, endeavour with our estates and lives, mutually to preserve the Rights and Priviledges of the Parliaments, and the Liberties of the kingdomes, and to preserve and defend the kings Maiesties person and authority, in the preservation and defence of the true Religion, and Liberties of the kingdomes, that the World may beare witnesse with our consciences of our Loyaltie, and that we have no thoughts or intentions to diminish his Maiesties iust power and greatnesse.

The Lord will Create upon every dwelling place of Mount Sion, & upon her Assemblies

a Cloud and smoke by day, and a shining of a flaming Fire by night, for upon all the glory shall be a defense. Isaiah 4. 5.

House of Lords   *House of Comons*

IV. We shall also with all faithfulnesse endeavour the discovery of all such as have beene, or shall be Incendiaries, Malignants, or evill Instruments, by hindering the Reformation of Religion, dividing the king from his people, or one of the kingdoms from another, or making any Faction or parties amongst the people, contrary to this league & Covenant, that they may be brought to publick triall, and receive condigne punishment, as the degree of their offences shall require or deserve, or the supream Iudicatories of both Kingdoms respectively, or others having power from them for that effect, shall iudge covenient.

I will purge out from among you the Rebells, & them that transgresse against me.

I will bring them forth out of the Countrey where they soiourne. Ezechiel. 20. 38. & 38.

A Malignant   *A Priest*

V.

And whereas the happinesse of a blessed Peace between these kingdoms, denyed in former times to our Progenitors, is by the good Providence of God granted unto us, and hath been lately concluded and settled by both Parliaments, we shall each one of us, according to our place and interest, indeavour that they may remain conioyned in a firm Peace an Union to all posterity; And that Justice may be done upon the wilfull Opposers thereof, in manner expressed in the precedent Article.

A threfold corde is not easily broken.

England   *Scotland*   *Ireland*

VI. We shall also according to our places & callings in this common cause of Religion, Liberty, and Peace of the kingdomes, assist and defend all those that enter into this League and Covenant, in the maintaining & pursuing thereof, and shall not suffer our selves directly or indirectly by whatsoever combination, perswasion or terror, to be devided & withdrawn from this blessed Union & coniunction, whether to make defection to the contrary part, or to give our selves to a detestable indifferency or neutrality in this cause which so much concerneth the glory of God, the good of the Kingdoms, and honour of the King; but shall all the dayes of our lives zealously and constantly continue therein, against all opposition, and promote the same according to our power, against all Lets and impediments whatsoever; an what we are not able our selves to suppresse or overcome, we shall reveale and make known, that it may be timely prevented or removed: All which we shall do as in the sight of God.

And his heart shall be against the holy Covenant. Dan: 11. 28.

And because these kingdoms are guilty of many sins & provocations against God, & his Son Iesus Christ, as is too manifest by our present distresses and dangers the fruits thereof, We professe and declare before God and the world, our unfayned desire to be humbled for our sins, & for the sins of these kingdoms, especially that we have not as we ought, valued the inestimable benefit of the Gospel, that we have not laboured for the purity and power thereof, and that we have not endeavored to receive Christ in our hearts, nor to walk worthy of him in our lives, which are the causes of other sins and transgressions, so much abounding amongst us, And our true and unfayned purpose desire, and endeavour for our selves, and all others under our power and charge, both in publick and in private, in all duties we owe to God and man, to amend our lives and each one to go before another in the Example of a reall Reformation, that the Lord may turne away his wrath, and heavy indignation, and establish these Churches and kingdoms in truth and peace. And this Covenant we make in the presence of almighty God, the Searcher of all hearts, with a true intention to performe the same, as we shall answer at that great day when the secrets of all hearts shall be disclosed. Most humbly beseeching the Lord to strengthen us by his Holy Spirit for this end, and to blesse our desires and proceedings with such successe, as may be deliverance and safety to his people, & encouragement to other Christian Churches groaning under or in danger of the yoake of Anti-christian Tyranny, to ioyne in the same, or like Association and Covenant, to the glory of God, the enlargement of the kingdome of Iesus Christ, and the peace and tranquility of Christian Kingdoms & Commonwealths.

Come & let us goe up to the mountaine of the Lord, & to the house of the God of Iacob; he will teach us of his wayes, & we will walke in his paths. Micah 4. 2.

Printed for Thomas Ienner

was his cousin, Edward Whalley, his own son Oliver, his nephew the younger Valentine Walton, and James Berry, a sectary, employed in his youth at an iron foundry in the western midlands, who was to prove himself indeed a 'man of a spirit'.

During 1643 Oliver Cromwell began to reveal his genius as a soldier. He proved to be not only a brave commander (in one battle he had his horse killed under him) but also a capable organizer, constantly badgering local sympathizers to provide pay and arms for his men. While the Earl of Essex remained overall commander-in-chief, the Committee of Safety, which looked after military affairs on behalf of parliament, formed associations of counties for mutual defence. Cambridgeshire and later Huntingdonshire were included in what was known as the Eastern Association and it was here that Oliver operated, preventing 'by his diligence the designs of the royal party.' Not content merely to act on the defensive, he wanted to invade Nottinghamshire and Lincolnshire to the north of the Eastern Association and link up with Lord Fairfax and his son Sir Thomas, two members of a family with fighting traditions, who were hard pressed by the Royalists in Yorkshire. But Oliver suffered from the failure of other colonels to co-operate with him and he was unfairly blamed by Essex for allowing the Queen, who had been collecting munitions in Holland, to arrive safely from Yorkshire and join her husband in Oxford, after skirting the borders of the Eastern Association.

Apart from that, the Parliamentarian campaign in the east of England was successful. A Royalist advance south from Yorkshire was checked by Oliver at the battle of Gainsborough in July and, although Lincolnshire was temporarily abandoned to the enemy, by October the Royalists were driven out again after a cavalry fight at Winceby where Oliver fought alongside Sir Thomas Fairfax. Oliver earned the nickname of Old Ironsides and won a considerable local reputation. After it had been decided at the end of the campaign to form an army under the Earl of Manchester to serve outside the confines of the Eastern Association, Cromwell was appointed to be his second in command with the rank of lieutenant-general; he was also appointed a member of the Committee of Both Kingdoms, which was formed out of the leading Parliamentarians and representatives of the Scots who, as a result of John Pym's diplomatic efforts before his death in December 1643, became allied with them in a 'Solemn League and Covenant'.

The Scottish alliance was thought necessary to defeat the King's armies because during 1643, outside the Eastern Association, the Royalists had been victorious nearly everywhere. Though at the opening of the campaign the Earl of Essex had captured Reading, thus menacing the King's headquarters at Oxford, by September he was compelled to abandon it. In Yorkshire the Fairfaxes were defeated and

Queen Henrietta Maria: a painting by Anthony van Dyck. Cromwell was accused of failing to prevent the Queen from joining her husband at Oxford after she had been in the United Netherlands to raise supplies for the Royalist army

(*Opposite*) an engraving of The Solemn League and Covenant (1643). This was the agreement between the English parliament and the Scottish Presbyterians for a military alliance in return for which the parliament promised to align its religion with that of the Scots. Oliver Cromwell was one of the last Englishmen to sign this agreement

25

The most Illustrious and High borne PRINCE RUPERT,
PRINCE ELECTOR, Second Son to FREDERICK
KING of BOHEMIA, GENERALL of the HORSE
of His MAJESTIES ARMY, KNIGHT of the Noble
Order of the GARTER.

(*Above and opposite*) Prince Rupert
of the Rhine, the ablest of Charles
I's generals and a great admirer of
Oliver Cromwell's military genius.
(*Below*) seventeenth-century
cavalry in formation and action

Prince Rupert, the King's young nephew, a professional soldier,
occupied Bristol in the west of England. The relief of Gloucester during August by a force led from London by the Earl of Essex was the
only notable Parliamentarian success; and then Essex had to cut his
way past the King's army in order to return safely to the capital.

Why were Cromwell's troopers victorious when the main armies
under Essex sustained defeats? The answer is partly that he was
selective in his recruiting. His men were 'honest sober Christians' and
were described as being 'of greater understanding than common
soldiers.' His officers were chosen for their merits rather than their
social standing. 'I had rather have,' wrote Oliver, 'a plain russet-
coated captain that knows what he fights for and loves what he knows,
than that which you call "a gentleman" and is nothing else.' Oliver
spared no pains in training his cavalrymen; he taught them how to
care for their horses and clean their weapons. Above all, regular drill
and strict discipline made his cavalry more manœuvrable than that of
Prince Rupert, whose troopers were dashing and daring but easily
got out of hand.

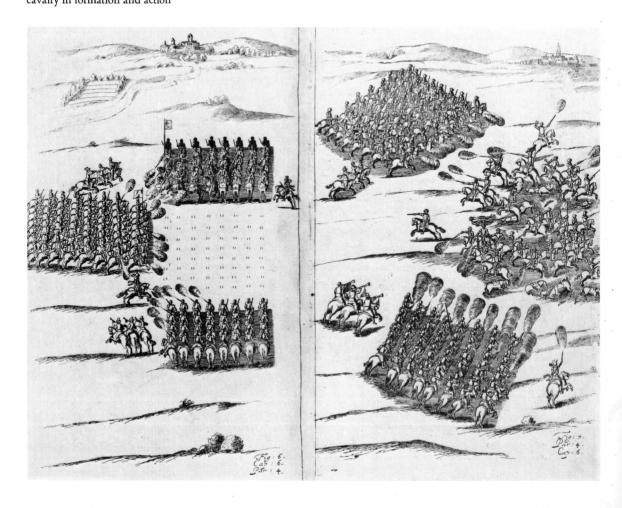

Royalist soldiers.
A musketeer (*top*) and a
cavalryman in full armour

During 1643 Oliver was absorbed in warfare; but he was also a member of parliament who had sprung into prominence just before the war began. After the Royalists had withdrawn from the House of Commons to join the King in Oxford, the two hundred or so members that remained were divided roughly into three groups. There was a peace group, headed by Denzil Holles, a member for Dorchester, who wanted the King, as soon as he had been taught a lesson, to be amicably restored to power; there was a war group led by young Harry Vane and a wealthy Leicestershire squire, Sir Arthur Haselrig, which was determined to go on fighting until the King was compelled to sue for the terms dictated to him and assume the position of a constitutional monarch, a mere ornamental figurehead. Thirdly, a middle group existed which was prepared to negotiate with the King on the basis that he accept parliamentary nomination of his ministers and reduce the power of the bishops. It is a mistake to call these political groupings 'parties'; at the most they consisted of twenty or thirty members; and some country gentlemen and lawyers trimmed between the peace and war groups. Oliver, though he was a radical where religion was concerned, was associated politically with the middle group to which his friends John Pym, Oliver St John and John Hampden belonged. In 1643 both Pym and Hampden died (the latter killed in an obscure skirmish) and St John took over the leadership of this middle group to which Oliver continued to adhere.

But the Scottish alliance was a new political factor. As a price for their military assistance the Scottish leaders had insisted that the English Church should be reformed along Presbyterian lines. Oliver, being a religious Independent or Congregationalist, wanted, as did Harry Vane, toleration for all Christian sects. Oliver was also convinced that a properly trained and carefully recruited Parliamentarian army was perfectly capable of defeating the King without the aid of the Scots. Thus the middle group and the war group drew together and were supported by the religious Independents. During 1644 a demand for religious toleration and a dislike of the behaviour of the Scots cemented an alliance between Manchester's army, largely picked and trained by Cromwell, the Independent divines, some of whom were chaplains in that army, and the war group and middle group in parliament led respectively by Oliver's friends, Vane and St John. Members of this composite party became dominant for a time: it was they who were to fashion what was known as the New Model Army, the instrument of the Parliamentarian victory over the King after the military setbacks in 1643 and, to a lesser extent, in 1644.

Oliver's immediate superior, the second Earl of Manchester, although he was one of the six members whom Charles I had attempted to arrest for treason, was in fact sympathetic to the peace group and owed his position less to his capacities as a soldier than to his noble

Edward Montagu, second Earl of Manchester, who was Oliver Cromwell's superior officer in 1643 and 1644, but was criticized by him as being lethargic and lacking the will for full victory over Charles I

rank; he was described as 'a sweet, meek man' who 'permitted his Lieutenant-General . . . to guide all the army at his pleasure'. Manchester's views tended towards Presbyterianism, but he admitted that two-thirds of his army were not of that faith but were Independents and sectaries. He also experienced the jealousy of the Earl of Essex, though he too belonged to the peace group, but resented the existence of a more or less separate command. Oliver and Harry Vane, on the other hand, disliked the Scottish alliance because they feared it meant the fastening upon the kingdom of a rigid Presbyterian system as provided for in the Solemn League and Covenant which every Englishman on the side of parliament was obliged to observe; it was significant that Oliver himself (and Oliver St John) did not take the oath to obey the Covenant until the last possible moment.

A contemporary caricature of Parliamentarian soldiers desecrating churches by pulling down paintings and moving altars. The Puritan iconoclasm was greatly exaggerated by the Royalists and later historians

Sir James Lumsden's recently discovered plan of the layout of the Parliamentary and Scottish armies at the battle of Marston Moor, when Lumsden was Major-General of the Foot. It shows the Allies divided into three bodies, Cromwell commanding cavalry on the left. Peter Young, in his book *Marston Moor*, estimates that according to this plan the Parliamentarian army consisted of about 21,200 men, i.e., 12,200 foot, 8,000 cavalry and 1,000 dragoons, but thinks this was an underestimate

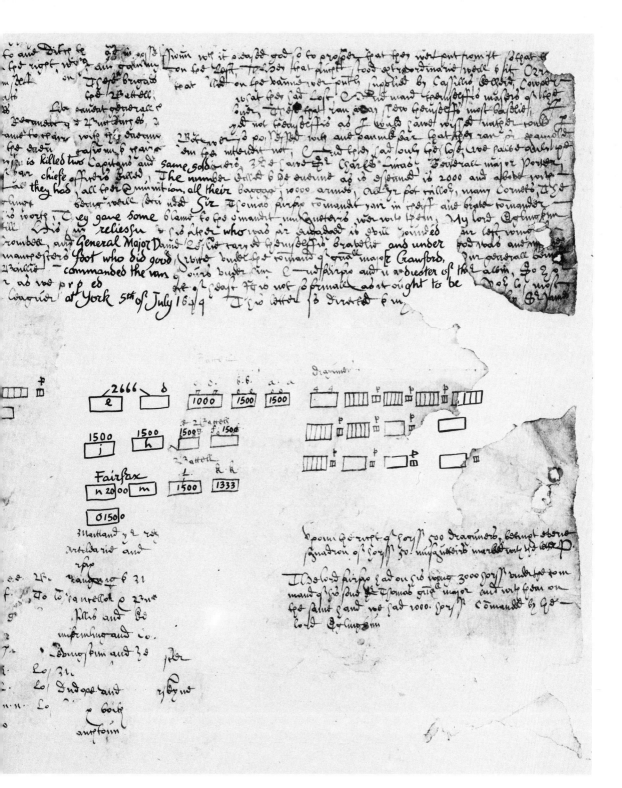

at York 5th of July 1644

2666

1000 1500 1500

1500 1500 1500 1500

Fairfax
2000 1500 1333

0150 0

A seventeenth-century engraving of the city of York, which was besieged by the Parliamentarians, relieved by Prince Rupert and then retaken after the battle of Marston Moor

Alexander Leslie, first Earl of Leven, who was the overall commander at the battle of Marston Moor

In May 1644 Manchester's army stormed Lincoln – Lincolnshire had been added to the Eastern Association on Cromwell's proposal – and then marched to join the Scottish army and the Fairfaxes in the siege of York, which was regarded as the northern capital of England. Charles I sent Prince Rupert to relieve York and immediately afterwards the Royalist army under his command confronted the three armies that had been taking part in the siege of York on the field of Marston Moor outside the city. Here the Royalists were outnumbered, but Rupert was determined to fight. Oliver was given the command of the Parliamentarian left wing with a cavalry force of 3,000 Englishmen from Manchester's army and some 1,500 Scottish cavalry and dragoons. The Scottish Earl of Leven, who was in supreme command, decided to order an attack at seven o'clock in the evening of 2 July. That was not playing the game according to the usual rules and Rupert was completely taken by surprise.

As soon as the signal had been given Oliver headed a charge with his first line and riding downhill forced his way across a ditch and through a hedge which had bounded the Royalist defensive position. Prince Rupert, who was sitting at supper when the battle began, himself directed a counter-charge. Although Oliver received a slight neck wound he rallied the second line and was assisted by a flank charge with his third line commanded by the Scots officer David Leslie. He also received support from the Scottish dragoons on his left under the command of Colonel Hugh Fraser and by the left wing of the Parliamentarian infantry on his right commanded by another Scotsman, Major-General Laurence Crawford. The Royalist infantry

elsewhere more or less held their ground and the Royalist cavalrymen who faced Sir Thomas Fairfax's Yorkshiremen on the Parliamentarian right were victorious. Fairfax bravely rode right across the battlefield to ask for Cromwell's help. After his own victory Oliver halted his men in excellent order – no easy feat of generalship – and then led his troopers over the moor to restore the position on the right and finally turned to the aid of the Parliamentarian infantrymen in the centre who had been broken but not beaten.

Owing to the initial failure of the infantry in the centre, the three leading generals, the Earl of Leven, the Earl of Manchester and Lord Fairfax, had given up all for lost. Though Oliver's Presbyterian critics tried to assign the victory to Leslie or Crawford (no contemporary attributed it to Sir Thomas Fairfax), Oliver first won a national reputation as a general for his conduct at Marston Moor because not only had he directed operations skilfully while his superiors were losing their heads, but also he had personally trained the troopers who turned the course of the battle.

After Marston Moor, Manchester hurried his men back home to the eastern counties and stubbornly refused to take any further offensive action. When one of his officers, Lieutenant-Colonel John Lilburne (the future leader of the individualist group nicknamed the Levellers), disobeyed orders by laying siege to a castle in Royalist hands, Manchester reproved him. When Oliver suggested that Manchester should attack the key town of Newark, he was ignored. When the Committee of Both Kingdoms ordered him to march against Prince Rupert, who was then attacking Chester, Manchester disobeyed.

A siege-piece cast by the Royalists at Newark in 1645

While Oliver was openly resentful over Manchester's slowness and inertia, he was also at cross purposes with Crawford, who was sufficiently aggressive and offensive, but employed his aggression and offensiveness largely by trying to discipline and even discharge the sectaries in Manchester's army. Oliver actually asked Manchester to dismiss Crawford on the ground that all his other colonels would otherwise resign. These internal squabbles induced the Committee of Both Kingdoms to summon Manchester, Cromwell and Crawford to Westminster. Oliver then withdrew his demand for Crawford's dismissal and was pacified by Manchester's promise to take action in the west of England.

Oliver's genuine willingness at this stage to soothe the Presbyterians was evidenced by his sending home one of the most outspoken of the Independent chaplains, William Dell, and even offering to accept in his place a minister nominated by the synod then meeting at Westminster which was overwhelmingly Presbyterian.

After the disaster at Marston Moor, Charles himself had led another Royalist army to the west of England and defeated the Earl of Essex in Cornwall. This royal victory perturbed the Committee of Both Kingdoms, for it offset Marston Moor. Manchester was ordered to join up with the remnants of the western armies and help to bar the King's return to his headquarters at Oxford. But the Parliamentarian army, which had no commander-in-chief and was instead directed by a Council of War, failed in its task. The King got back safely to Oxford after defying the Parliamentarians at what was known as the second battle of Newbury. After the battle Oliver still wanted to attack the King and spoke in this sense at the Council of War. Manchester then said: 'If we beat the King ninety-nine times, yet he is King still, but if the King beat us once we shall all be hanged.' 'My Lord,' retorted Oliver, 'if this be so why did we take up arms at first? This is against fighting ever hereafter.'

By this time Oliver had lost all patience with the attitude of Essex and Manchester and the peace group in parliament. At the end of November 1644 he returned to the House of Commons and delivered a series of speeches criticizing the whole conduct of the war. Without difficulty he won the support of the leaders of the war group, such as Harry Vane and Arthur Haselrig. He openly attacked his own commander-in-chief and in his temper expressed the wish that there was no longer a nobleman in England. After he recovered his temper, he admitted that he himself was guilty of oversights in military matters. Then he said: 'I hope we have such true English hearts and zealous affections towards the general weal of our Mother Country, as no members of either House will scruple to deny themselves and their own private interests for the general good.'

This was the germ of the proposal put forward by the war group

34

and middle group in the Commons to exclude all members of either House of Parliament from future service in the armed forces and to create a new army. Enthusiasm gripped the Commons; Vane offered to resign his lucrative post of Treasurer of the Navy; on 19 December a Self-Denying Ordinance was unanimously voted; and Oliver was appointed to a committee to draw up a scheme for a New Model Army. On 21 January 1645 Sir Thomas Fairfax, who was not a member of parliament, was chosen by a majority of 101 to 69 to command the new army, Cromwell and Vane acting as tellers for the affirmative. But it was not for another month that the remnant of the House of Lords finally and reluctantly acquiesced in these arrangements. For they meant the end of the road for the Earls of Essex and Manchester, the peace-group procrastinators.

Although Oliver was to have nothing to do with the actual organization and training of the New Model Army, which was the task of the commander-in-chief, Fairfax, and of the major-general in charge of the infantry, the experienced Phillip Skippon, an old professional soldier of fanatical Puritan bent who had risen from the ranks, he was actively concerned with the planning stage. He pressed the view that Fairfax should be allowed to choose his own officers, subject to parliamentary approval, and that they should not be nominated by parliament; he was against every soldier being obliged to swear his loyalty to the Solemn League and Covenant in front of the army commanders; he was a prominent member of the committee charged with recruiting the army; and he was appointed to another committee involved in borrowing money from the City of London to pay for the immediate needs of the new army.

(*Left*) a satirical medal of Sir Thomas Fairfax, the commander-in-chief of the New Model Army, and (*right*) a portrait attributed to Edward Bower. Oliver Cromwell loyally served under Fairfax from 1645 to 1650. Fairfax had Royalist sympathies, was opposed to Charles I's execution and in the end helped the restoration of King Charles II

THE PARLIAMENTARIAN SOLDIER

(*Left*) uniform of a trooper and (*right*) statuette of a trooper

(*Below*) a priming flask, and devices worn by Parliamentarian officers

(*Opposite*) print of a painted glass window from Farndon church, Cheshire, showing the cavaliers at Chester

The DEVISES *MOTTO's &c. used by the* Parliament Officers *on* STANDARDS, BANNE &c. in the late CIVIL WARS; taken from an Original Manuscript done at y̓ time now in y̓ hands of ja͡ Cole of Oxford. Published at y̓ Desire of divers Gentlemen to be Bound up w͡ y̓ Lord Clarendon's H

Ora et Pugna Juvet et Juvabit JEHOVAH

Lex Suprema Salus Patriæ

Only in Heaven

One of Thise

My Oath and Sword Maintain this Word

Pro Rege Lege &

Maj͡ C.Skinner one of the Comittie for y̓ Militia and Cap͡ of a Troop of Horse 1642

Cap͡ Harvie Cap͡ of the City Tredbands and Cap͡ of a Troop of Horse 1642

Cap͡ Mannwaring one of y̓ City Cap͡ and Cap͡ of a Troop of Horse 1642

Cap͡ Brown one of y̓ City Capt and Cap͡ of a Troop of Horse & Coll͡ of a Reg͡ of Dragoons 1642

Captain Welborne Cap͡ of a Troop of Horse 1642

Cap͡ Withers

36

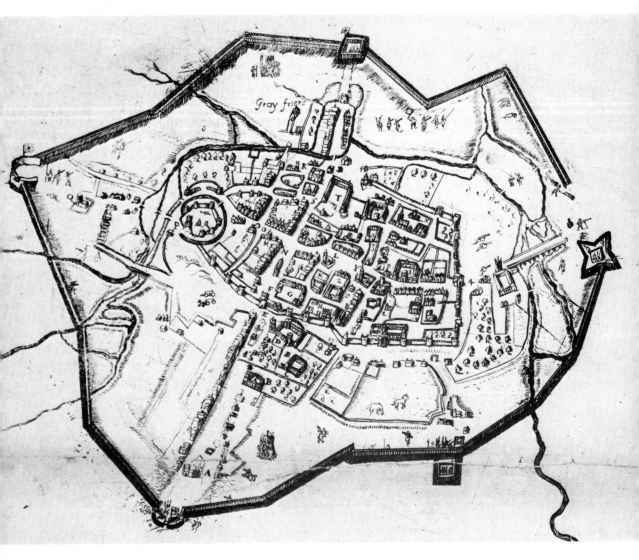

Gray fryers

A map of Oxford and its
fortifications as they were when the
city was the Royalist headquarters
in 1644

The Self-Denying Ordinance, finally agreed to on 3 April 1645,
gave members of parliament forty days' grace before they needed to
lay down their commissions. Thus, pending the formation of the new
army, Sir William Waller and Oliver Cromwell as his second in
command were instructed to ride with a cavalry force to the west of
England where the Royalists were still strong. Nothing much came
of this campaign in the early spring and on 17 April Oliver was
ordered to surrender his commission to Fairfax. Fairfax was a great
admirer of Cromwell's abilities as a cavalry officer; they had fought
side by side at Winceby and in the last stages of the battle of Marston
Moor. Fairfax deliberately left vacant the post of lieutenant-general
responsible for the cavalry in the New Model Army. It can scarcely

be doubted that, despite the Self-Denying Ordinance, he wanted Oliver for the post.

At any rate, instead of delivering up his commission Oliver was assigned the task of watching the King's movements in Oxford, while Fairfax, acting under the orders of the Committee of Both Kingdoms, took his New Model Army into the south-west. Before Fairfax set out he conferred with Oliver and gave him reinforcements so that he could isolate the King in Oxford. Oliver went energetically to work. But though he had several successes to the south of Oxford, he was unable to prevent Charles from moving out to the north along the Woodstock road. Fairfax was satisfied that Oliver was doing his best and on 10 May requested the House of Commons to extend Oliver's commission for another forty days, that is to say until 22 June. After Fairfax was recalled from a fruitless expedition to relieve Taunton, he himself took over the siege of Oxford and ordered Oliver back to the Eastern Association where he held the position of governor of the Isle of Ely. His sending Oliver home did not mean that Fairfax wanted to get rid of him. For no one knew what Charles's plans might be; he could be trying to go north to attack the Scots or he might be intending to assault the Parliamentarian strongholds in the east midlands or East Anglia. In fact at the end of May Charles I and Prince Rupert stormed the city of Leicester, sparing few of the garrison and plundering the city.

The Committee of Both Kingdoms now realized that it had better give up amateur strategy and leave the military decisions to the generals in the field. Fairfax was therefore allowed to lift the siege of Oxford and do what he thought fit. He decided to try to bring Charles I's army in the midlands to battle before it could receive reinforcements from the west. Fairfax urgently dispatched a messenger to Ely ordering Oliver to join him and at the same time asked parliament to approve Oliver's appointment as lieutenant-general in charge of the cavalry. Oliver promptly rode at the head of six hundred men to meet Fairfax and on 14 June he took command of the right wing at the battle of Naseby where the Royalist army was outnumbered and almost completely destroyed. After three hours King Charles reluctantly abandoned the field and Fairfax and Cromwell marched to the west to defeat the last intact Royalist army at the battle of Langport on 10 July. Thus was the New Model Army blooded.

When the New Model Army was first formed, its establishment was for 22,000 men, but many other Parliamentarian forces were scattered about the country. These were ultimately to be absorbed into the New Model which thus became a national army under the command of Fairfax. It also acquired a distinct character of its own, counterbalancing the Presbyterians who held sway at Westminster and the peace group in parliament.

(*Overleaf*) the layout of the forces of the Royalists and Parliamentarians at the battle of Naseby in June 1645: an engraving from Joshua Sprigge, *Anglia Rediviva* (1647). The portrait in the right-hand top corner is that of Fairfax. Cromwell commanded the cavalry on the right wing, his son-in-law, Henry Ireton, commanded the left wing, also cavalry. The infantry are shown massed in the centre

THE DESCRIPTION OF THE ARMIES OF HO...
Sr Thomas Fairefax his Excellency, as they were drawn ...
the Fowerteen...

40

AND FOOT OF HIS MAJESTIES, AND
everall bodyes, at the Battayle at NASBYE;
ay of June 1645

Hugh Peter, a Parliamentarian chaplain and a great admirer of Oliver Cromwell whom he served in various capacities

A portrait believed to be that of William Dell, Master of Gonville and Caius College, Cambridge, from 1649 to 1660. Dell was chaplain-in-chief in the Parliamentarian army from the beginning of 1646

Unquestionably the independent character of the army was due directly or indirectly to Oliver and his friends, the sectarian ministers. Although over half the New Model consisted of pressed men, not volunteers, the core of the army were soldiers who had served in Manchester's army, raised and trained by Oliver in East Anglia, the only army that had never been beaten. The ordinary infantrymen were divided in their political and religious opinions but the cavalry, who were both of higher social status and better paid, were almost all sectaries or Independents who sought toleration and not adherence to a rigid Presbyterian Church. Most of the Presbyterian chaplains had left the army after the battle of Edgehill, but in 1645 a number of enthusiastic chaplains attached themselves to Fairfax's headquarters.

These new chaplains included William Dell, Oliver's friend, whom he had sent away at the end of 1643 to pacify the Earl of Manchester, and Hugh Peter, a militant Independent and contemporary of Oliver at Cambridge, who 'rode from rank to rank with a Bible in one hand and a sword in the other exhorting the men to do their duty.' Other experienced Independent chaplains who served with the new army were William Erbury, William Sedgwick and John Saltmarsh. Most of them had been educated at Puritan colleges in Cambridge. Edward Bowles, the last Presbyterian chaplain and an intimate friend of Fairfax, departed after the battle of Naseby and was replaced as the leading minister at Fairfax's headquarters by William Dell. Dell and Peter both attacked the Presbyterians in their sermons; to offset the growing influence of these sectarians, Richard Baxter, an extremely able minister of a Presbyterian frame of mind, thought it his duty to join the New Model Army in the capacity of chaplain to the regiment commanded by Oliver's cousin, Edward Whalley. But Baxter was dismayed by what he saw. Cromwell, he said, 'coldly bid me welcome and never spoke one word to me more while I was there.' He thought that Fairfax was one whom Cromwell could 'make use of at his pleasure'. He perceived that while many honest Christians were to be found in the army, the most active and persuasive were Baptists and the like, who followed Oliver in insisting upon liberty of conscience. The new chaplains gradually acquired an extraordinary power over the men, preaching to them every Sabbath day and on the eve of battles. 'As the official spokesmen for the army, the chaplains were both to influence and to reflect the point of view of Cromwell and the headquarters staff, particularly in reference to religious matters.' (Leo F. Solt) They also preached in the towns to which the army marched. They received support from unordained or lay preachers whose sermons so alarmed the House of Commons that Fairfax was ordered to forbid their meetings. Peter thought that the men of the New Model were more religious than any. Saltmarsh felt certain that 'God is amongst us.'

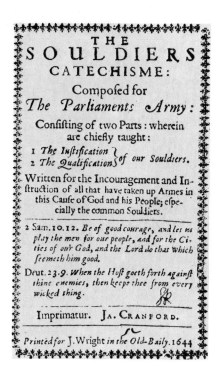

(*Left*) title-page of the *Souldier's Catechism* (1644). There was also a pocket Bible used in the Parliamentarian armies

(*Right*) opening page of The New Common Prayer Book, 1644, with an ordinance of parliament for the abolition of the Book of Common Prayer and for putting into force the Directory for the Worship of God. This Directory was drawn up by the Presbyterians

To Dell the victories of the New Model were 'the works of the Lord' wrought by 'the Saints of God' in whose hearts the Holy Spirit resided. The religious inspiration and individualistic temper of the chaplains earned the approval of Oliver who, according to Manchester, had been determined from the first to have none in the army but such as were of Independent judgment. Later in life Oliver came to wonder if this Army of Saints might indeed be a lawful power called by God not merely to serve but to rule.

The battle of Naseby did not end the first civil war. Charles I, an incorrigible optimist, believed that the whole of the west of England was still loyal to him and hoped to recruit a new army in Wales. For nearly a year after the battle of Langport, Thomas Fairfax and Oliver Cromwell were fully occupied in reducing the west to obedience to parliament. While they were there, Charles actually made a sortie from Oxford and plundered Oliver's birthplace of Huntingdon. Oliver's commission as lieutenant-general was twice extended: in August 1645 for four months and in January 1646 for a further six months. During that time he took part in the successful siege of Devizes, he stormed the almost impregnable Basing House further east, he was present at the fall of Dartmouth in Devon and he super-vised the surrender of Exeter. The south-west of England having been largely cleared of Royalist troops, Oliver accompanied Thomas Fairfax to the blockade of Oxford which opened in May 1646.

An eighteenth-century engraving
of the house in Clerkenwell Close,
off Drury Lane, where Oliver
Cromwell was living with his
family in 1646

During this long campaign, lasting from the battle of Naseby to
the fall of Oxford, Oliver was deeply conscious not only of the
'providences of God' but also of the valiant conduct of the New
Model Army imbued with God's spirit. After Naseby he wrote to
the Speaker of the House of Commons telling him of the 'good hand
of God' but also reminding him that 'honest men served you faithfully in this action.' After Langport he praised God for giving the
victory to 'a company of poor ignorant men'; and after the surrender
of Bristol, while he insisted that only 'a very atheist' could deny that
it was the work of God, he stressed that this 'great business' had not
been performed by any one kind of Christian: 'Presbyterians,
Independents all had there the same spirit of faith and prayer . . .
pity it is it should be otherwise anywhere.' Following the storm of
Basing House he added a more practical point in his dispatch to the

a

b

c

d

Speaker: 'I must speak my judgment to you,' he wrote, if you intend to have your work carried on . . . a course [must be] taken to pay your army.'

During these months Oliver made only a short visit to London. But when Oxford surrendered in June 1646 he moved his family from Ely and set up house in Drury Lane: his family consisted of his wife, two of his sons, Richard and Henry, and two of his daughters, Mary and Frances. One of his sons, young Oliver, had died of smallpox during the war and two other daughters, Bridget and Elizabeth, were married. From that time on Oliver laid aside his sword and concentrated on his duties as a member of parliament. But he was still on the army pay roll and kept in close touch with the Commander-in-Chief, Thomas Fairfax, concerning himself in particular with the planning of an expeditionary force for the relief of Ireland.

(a) Richard Cromwell, who succeeded his father as Lord Protector in September 1658
(b) Mary Cromwell, Oliver's third daughter, who married Lord Fauconberg to please her parents. She was nicknamed Mall
(c) Frances Cromwell, Oliver's youngest daughter. Frances married – for love – Robert Rich, a grandson of the Earl of Warwick
(d) Bridget Cromwell, Oliver's eldest daughter. She twice married according to the wishes of her father, first Henry Ireton and second Charles Fleetwood

The majority in the House of Commons was extremely nervous about what the army might do now the war was over and resented its demands for a generous financial settlement and for religious toleration. It has in fact been claimed that from 1645 the radicals and Independents obtained control of the army at the same time as they lost control of parliament and the City of London. Thus an explosive situation was created. In August 1646 Cromwell was telling Fairfax: 'We are full of faction and worse', and in October he was warning him about a petition which parliament received from the City striking at the army. By March 1647 he was informing Fairfax: 'Never were the spirits of men more embittered than now. Surely the Devil hath but a short time', and in the same letter he asserted, 'there want not in all places men who have so much malice against the army as besots them.'

Parliament was now in fact divided into what may roughly be described as Presbyterian and Independent groupings. From 1645 to 1647 new members were being recruited to the House of Commons: this may not have materially altered the balance of the House, although some Independents were elected who might not have been at an earlier stage. The so-called Independent party from 1645 to 1648 has been described as an alliance between the old middle and war groups with firm ties with the army leadership; Oliver Cromwell was on friendly terms with both Oliver St John and Harry Vane and was in close contact with Fairfax. Meanwhile Charles I had escaped from Oxford before its surrender and presented himself at the headquarters of the Scottish army which had moved to Newark. By December 1646 parliament concluded a treaty with the Scots of a purely military character providing for the withdrawal of their army from England. It was signed among others by Cromwell and St John, but not by Vane. Oliver was taken ill early in 1647. By this time the Presbyterians, led by Denzil Holles and Sir Philip Stapleton, had secured a majority in the Commons. The King, who had been moved by the Scots to Newcastle, where he refused far-reaching proposals sent to him from Westminster, was handed over to the custody of the English parliament. But the army leaders naturally feared that an agreement damaging to religious freedom would be concluded between the parliamentary majority and Charles I.

As has been observed, the character of the New Model Army had been moulded since its formation in 1645 not so much by Cromwell or Fairfax as by the eloquent army chaplains like Dell and Peter. Just before the surrender of Oxford, Dell preached a sermon which caused something of a sensation. After the sermon he was asked by one of his audience if he thought all Presbyterians were 'carnal gospellers'. He replied that some of them were very godly Christians imbued with the spirit of the Lord. 'For my part,' he added, 'I do not allow any

nglands Miraculous Preſervation Emblematically Deſcribed, Erected

for a perpetuall *MONVMENT* to Poſterity.

Though Englands Ark haue furios storms jndurd
By Plotts of foes and power of the sword
Yet to this day by Gods almighty hand
The Ark's preservd and almost safe at land

(*Above*) a broadsheet
commemorating the Parliamentarian
victory in the first civil war with
drawings of the various generals,
including Cromwell in the
right-hand bottom corner.

(*Right*) a contemporary woodcut
showing Fairfax presiding over
a meeting of the Council of the
Army

Henry Ireton, Oliver Cromwell's friend and son-in-law

such distinction of Christians as Presbyterians and Independents, this being only a distinction of man's making, tending to the division of the Church'; he asserted further that 'as in Christ's kingdom neither circumcision availeth anything, nor uncircumcision, but a new creature.' For that sermon Dell was summoned before the House of Lords, presided over by Oliver's old superior, the Earl of Manchester, and was accused of saying that no authority could bind the Saints (that is the Independents) and that 'the power is in you the people'. Dell was acquitted, but Colonel John Lilburne, who was one of Dell's 'Saints', was fined and imprisoned.

Hugh Peter, who had accompanied Oliver during the campaign in the west, was even more outspoken than Dell. He was present at Bristol when Oliver wrote his long dispatch to the Speaker. He and Dell both preached before the siege of Dartmouth. Hugh Peter said in February that 'in the army there were twenty several opinions and they live quietly together'; he pleaded for unity to achieve religious and social reform; at Oxford he lashed out against the Scots; he boasted that he was an Independent and in a series of sermons during the summer of 1646 he preached to the army and to the City of London against the Presbyterians.

Not only Peter and Dell but other army chaplains, like Saltmarsh and Owen, were accused of preaching the 'wicked heresy' that all men are or can be saved. It is doubtful if in fact they did so. But they certainly believed that God gathered his Church out of the Elect, that the names of all sects and divisions ought to be laid aside, and that the magistrate had no right to dictate religious beliefs but only to secure the maintenance of law and order in society. That was the kind of thinking that prevailed in Cromwell's world and shaped his own outlook. It is notable that William Dell officiated at the wedding of Oliver's eldest daughter, Bridget, to Colonel Henry Ireton; that Oliver used Peter as his messenger to parliament; and that later he supported Owen's plan for Church reform on a liberal basis.

Oliver had been much happier with his friends in the army than he was in the House of Commons, although there too he had his own group of friends. Besides Vane and St John, officers from the army had been 'recruited' to the House: these included Oliver's new son-in-law, Henry Ireton, a man of high intelligence and a severe Puritan; Charles Fleetwood, an affable gentleman of Baptist persuasion who had commanded a cavalry regiment in the New Model Army; and Thomas Harrison, son of a butcher, who was the first major in Fleetwood's regiment and formerly a clerk in Clifford's Inn and an extreme sectarian. But the Presbyterians, most of whom belonged to the peace group, dominated the House, and Oliver found it less easy to have his own way there than he had done in the army. 'It was a miserable thing to serve in Parliament', he told Colonel Edmund

Ludlow, another 'recruited' member, 'to whom let a man never be so faithful if one pragmatical fellow amongst them rise up and asperse him, he shall never wipe it off. Whereas when one serves a General, he may do so as much service and yet be free from all blame and envy.'

Oliver assured the Commons that the army would disband if ordered to do so. But in his absence the New Model was growing more and more restless. Not only were the soldiers clamouring for their arrears of pay and compensation for their losses while in service and petitioning parliament in this sense, but they looked forward to the establishment of a new government which would ensure religious toleration and social reforms. John Lilburne, though now in prison (not for the first time) was in the process of creating a radical political movement largely by smuggling out of his cell virulent pamphlets which were secretly printed by his friends. Lilburne wanted freedom of speech and of the press, legal and prison reforms, the abolition of monopolies and tithes, and social legislation to benefit the poor. Lilburne's pamphlets were eagerly read in the army by the rank and file, especially by the cavalry troopers who treated them as gospel truths. He acquired the nickname of 'Freeborn John' and his followers were called Levellers. Whether or not under the influence of Leveller teaching, the privates in the army began demanding direct representation in the negotiations about their future which were taking place between the House of Commons and the army officers. Eight cavalry regiments were the first to elect such representatives or agents, who were commonly known as Agitators.

On 21 March 1647 commissioners from the Commons presented their proposals to the army which was stationed at Saffron Walden: they sought to find volunteers for service in an expeditionary force to go to Ireland and to secure the disbandment of the rest of the army on the receipt of four weeks' arrears of pay. The offer provoked doubts among the officers and anger among the soldiers. Oliver at first remained loyal to parliament and rejected the extreme demands of the soldiers. Since he had been voted an income of £2,500 a year in land for his services in the civil war, his disinterestedness was called into question. Lilburne wrote to Oliver accusing him of putting the army into the clutches of Holles and Stapleton and being 'led by the nose by two covetous earthworms, Vane and St John.' But in fact Oliver's sympathies were with the soldiers, more especially when on 30 March Holles succeeded in carrying a motion through the House of Commons that petitioners in the army were 'enemies of the State'.

The Parliamentarians were naturally perturbed by the attitude and temper of the army, and hesitated between firmness and concession. Finally in May they voted in favour of an improved offer and Oliver, together with his younger friends, Ireton and Fleetwood, and Major-General Phillip Skippon, who had been selected to head the Irish

The Sun Inn, Saffron Walden, reputedly used by the Parliamentarian army when it held meetings in that town in 1647

expeditionary force, were sent to Saffron Walden to put it before the army. Oliver delivered a speech in Saffron Walden church in which he did his best to induce the officers to accept the parliamentary votes and persuade their men to do so, but he was obliged to report back to the Speaker that he had found the army under a deep sense of grievance and when he returned to Westminster he expressed the opinion that though the army might agree to disband on reasonable terms, it would refuse to serve under Skippon in Ireland.

Therefore the Presbyterian leaders in the Commons abandoned concession. Instead they planned to negotiate with the Scots, to raise a new army in London, and to order the regiments of the New Model to disperse and disband. Ireton told Cromwell that he thought 'the disobliging of so faithful an army will be repented of.' It was rumoured that Oliver himself was going to be put under arrest. At any rate he felt that he had done all he could by way of conciliation and at the beginning of June he left his London home and joined the army in its new headquarters at Newmarket.

The army then decided to take measures for its own security. Acting in all probability on the advice of the Agitators, Cornet George Joyce (cornet being the lowest rank of officer) collected five hundred men to seize the artillery at Oxford and whisk King Charles I out of the hands of parliament. Whether Oliver gave his assent to Joyce's move is not clear, but when Joyce returned, bringing the King away from the house in Northamptonshire where he had been enjoying honourable captivity, to Childerley near Cambridge, Cromwell and Ireton interviewed him there and assured him that his kidnapping was not of their doing.

Events then moved rapidly. Two days after Cromwell met Charles I for the first time, parliamentary commissioners arrived at Cambridge and promised the army that its arrears would be paid in full. But the concession came too late. The Agitators distrusted the leaders in the Commons and believed that they were merely buying time while attempting to raise another army to fight against them. On 12 June the New Model Army advanced to St Albans, thus menacing London. On 14 June a declaration, drawn up by Ireton, asked that parliament should be 'purged' and a new House of Commons chosen, and accused eleven of the Presbyterian MPs of treason. The army had come to regard itself as a third force in the kingdom and Oliver and Henry Ireton, acting on its behalf, entered into negotiations with the King for a political settlement. But Charles, understandably rejoicing in the quarrel between the Commons and the New Model Army, was in no hurry to agree to terms for his own restoration to power. Moreover, he was distrustful of Cromwell and Ireton because they asked nothing for themselves. He tried to bribe Oliver with the offer of an earldom and the post of captain of his guards. Finally he sent

a letter to parliament asking that the army's proposals should be taken into consideration.

But already the army was getting out of hand. On 16 and 17 July a Council of the Army, including the Agitators and over a hundred officers, met at Reading under the presidency of General Fairfax, and he and Oliver were strongly pressed to lead a march into London so as to gain control of parliament. Oliver was extremely reluctant to give his consent. Though he admitted that he wanted to see a purged and reformed parliament, he was unwilling to obtain it by compulsion. He was anxious to avoid a second war and to gain what he thought was for the good of the kingdom without the use of force. For he still remained loyal to the policy of that middle group, first led by John Pym and then by St John, who wanted to negotiate an agreed settlement with the King. Yet Oliver's oratory proved of no avail. The rank and file insisted on direct action. When it was learned that a London mob had invaded the two Houses of Parliament demanding that the King should be invited to the City to accept a settlement based on the Solemn League and Covenant and that the Speaker and fifty-seven members of the House of Commons were fleeing from Westminster to seek refuge with the army, Oliver and

Major-General John Lambert, Cromwell's second in command at the battle of Preston

Hampton Court Palace. Charles I was kept as a prisoner there in honourable captivity in 1647. Cromwell frequently used it as his country home when he became Lord Protector

the other general officers felt obliged to give way. On 6 August, Fairfax brought his army up to London to restore order, thus compelling most of the Presbyterian leaders to depart abroad.

During the remainder of 1647 Oliver did his utmost to arrange a constitutional settlement between the King, parliament and the army. First of all, Oliver and Henry Ireton continued their negotiations with Charles I, which began at Childerley, went on at Woburn in Bedfordshire and were concluded in Hampton Court Palace where Charles took up residence, having given his parole not to escape, on 24 August. By that time the army had withdrawn from Westminster and was encamped on Putney Heath.

A statesmanlike scheme for a written constitution, known as the 'Heads of the Proposals', drafted by Ireton with the assistance of a highly intelligent twenty-eight-year-old colonel from Yorkshire named John Lambert (like Ireton he had been educated at Cambridge and the Inns of Court), had been accepted by the Council of Officers on 1 August. General Fairfax, who himself preferred to remain outside the political arena, appointed at the end of August a committee of officers, in which Cromwell and Ireton were the dominant figures, to deal with such questions. The King, who was far from averse to

dividing parliament from the army, sent daily messages from Hampton Court to Cromwell and Ireton when he was not actually interviewing them. Oliver was somewhat embarrassed by these attentions and begged Charles's emissary, Jack Ashburnham, 'not to come so frequently to his quarters but to send privately to him.' The negotiations aroused misgivings not only among the rank and file of the army, where the influence of the Levellers and Agitators was growing stronger all the time, but also in the House of Commons, for although the Presbyterian leaders were no longer there, a majority of the members was against coming to any settlement with the King except on the basis of the Church of England being transformed into a kind of Presbyterian Kirk, as provided for in the Solemn League and Covenant with the Scots agreed to in 1643.

Oliver, fully conscious that a cloud of suspicion lay over his actions, picked his way warily. He consented to the propositions of Newcastle, which had provided for a Presbyterian Church, being resubmitted to the King by parliament; he paid a visit to John Lilburne, the Leveller leader who was still imprisoned in the Tower of London, and begged him not to stir up trouble in the army; and he had expelled from the Army Council an officer who indiscreetly remarked that no visible authority was left in the kingdom but the power of the sword. When the King notified parliament that he preferred the 'Heads of the Proposals' to the 'Propositions of Newcastle', Oliver carried in the House of Commons a motion that a grand committee should be appointed to negotiate a personal treaty with the King. This motion was afterwards virtually rescinded when Oliver was away in Putney. Nevertheless, according to one account, Oliver promised the King that he would stand by him 'if there were but ten men left to stick by him.' At that time Charles I had no small hopes that Cromwell would restore him to power. Nor did Oliver conceal his own position. Though he was prepared to accept a temporary Presbyterian Church system, with toleration for the sects outside it, he said that he did not believe that the country could be happy and at peace unless the King enjoyed his rights. On 17 October he delivered a three-hour speech in the Commons urging that it was necessary to re-establish the King as quickly as possible.

But in the world in which Oliver was moving there were many conflicting and irreconcilable pressures. In the Commons a vociferous republican group had been formed, led by Henry Marten, who was reputed to be a 'whoremaster' and atheist. The Levellers came forward and offered Fairfax their own written constitution, providing for the dissolution of the existing parliament and its replacement by one that was more democratically elected and could govern the country without a King, House of Lords or Established Church. Thomas Harrison, now promoted a colonel, believed that the country would shortly be ruled by Jesus Christ returning to earth to set up a Fifth Monarchy and wanted the King to be put on trial as a Man of Blood.

During the fortnight beginning on 28 October 1647, a series of meetings of what was known as the General Council of the Army took place at Putney to try to thrash out an agreed plan. In it were not only the higher officers but the current Agitators and two civilian representatives of the Levellers. Fairfax was conveniently ill most of the time and the chair was taken by Oliver who insisted that he had no preconceived ideas and vainly tried to harmonize all the conflicting views. Henry Ireton was opposed to a more democratic constitution, which he thought would lead to anarchy and communism, and insisted that the army was committed by its earlier engagements to try to reach an understanding with the King. After the tide of opinion in the General Council of the Army had turned against Ireton to such an extent that Oliver was obliged to allow the discussion of a republican solution, he and his son-in-law decided that the whole situation was out of hand. They persuaded Fairfax to order the Agitators back to their regiments; they told Colonel Thomas Harrison that they were against the trial of the King; the meetings of the army were broken up and then held in three different areas; and a mutiny in two regiments was suppressed, Oliver himself seizing hold of the ringleaders who were tried by court martial and condemned to death: they drew lots and one of them was shot.

Oliver was so alarmed by the temper in the army that he wrote to his cousin, Colonel Edward Whalley, who was responsible for the King's safety at Hampton Court, warning him that an attempt might be made on Charles 1's life. Whalley rather foolishly showed the letter to the King who used it as an excellent excuse to break his parole and escape. But Charles had no thought-out scheme whether to make for Scotland, try to obtain a ship for France, there to join his Queen, or to find a haven in the Isle of Wight where he hoped he might be able to negotiate for his restoration free from pressures of parliament or army. It was not until two days after his escape that the King, who had found shelter in the house of the Earl of Southampton at Titchfield, finally decided that he would go to the Isle of Wight. The idea which was later bruited about, that Oliver with Machiavellian cunning had somehow wafted him there, is absurd.

Oliver's main concern in the late autumn of 1647 was to keep the army united. Not only had he to cope with mutiny and dissension in the ranks, but he needed to pacify the colonels. His son-in-law Ireton became increasingly distrustful of the King since his flight from Hampton Court; Colonel Edmund Ludlow was advocating republicanism and Colonel Thomas Rainsborough democracy; the former colonel, John Lilburne, wanted annual parliaments and the House of Commons made clearly responsible to the electorate;

Charles I with Colonel Robert Hammond, the Governor of the Isle of Wight: a woodcut of 1648. The King escaped to the Isle of Wight from Hampton Court in November 1647

Carisbrooke Castle as it was in the seventeenth century and as it is today. Charles I was kept a prisoner there until he was brought back to Westminster for his trial in 1649

Colonel Robert Hammond, who was related by marriage to the Cromwells, was understandably agitated because as Governor of the Isle of Wight he had to accept the unenviable responsibility of guarding the King when he took up residence in Carisbrooke Castle.

On 19 November, Oliver assured the Commons that although attempts had been made to seduce the army, it was loyal and united, but added that the soldiers were asserting that as citizens they possessed the right to petition about their grievances; on 23 November in another speech, he blamed the Levellers for trying to thrust the army into folly and said that he 'could not but disclaim and discountenance such endeavours' which 'brought so many obloquies upon him and the officers.' In fact by the end of the year he was on more friendly terms with the Levellers; the mutineers who had been imprisoned were released; and Colonel Rainsborough was shrewdly offered the command of the fleet to take him out of harm's way.

Meanwhile Charles I's intrigues in the Isle of Wight helped Oliver in his aim of uniting the army, pacifying the House of Commons and conciliating the City of London. After terms offered by the King had been more or less rejected by parliament, he entered into negotiations with commissioners from Scotland who were prepared to engage themselves to send an army into England for the purpose of restoring him to power if he would agree to their terms, including the introduction of Presbyterianism in England and special favours for Scotland. At the same time a Royalist reaction was taking place in England partly owing to the failure of parliament to achieve a political settlement but mainly because the existing government was blamed for economic distress resulting from successive bad harvests.

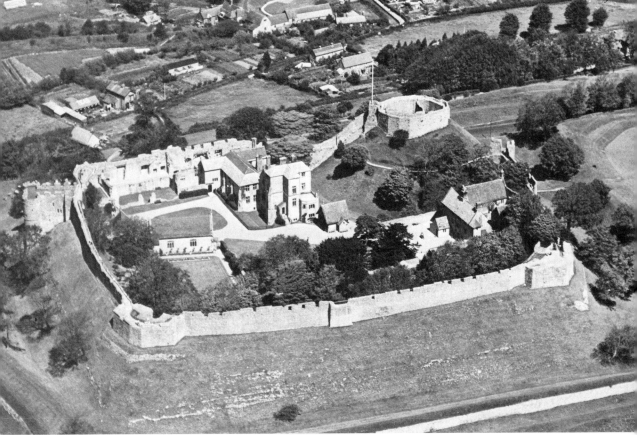

Pembroke Castle: a photograph
of it as it is today and a seventeenth-
century drawing. Cromwell
besieged and took the castle at the
beginning of the second civil war

The news that Charles I was exploiting the social unrest and general
uncertainty in his two kingdoms caused Oliver to take action. The
radical group and the middle group in the Commons united to carry
by 141 votes to 92 a resolution that no more negotiations should be
entered into with the King. In his speech Oliver insisted that while he
still supported monarchy in principle 'unless necessity enforce an
alteration', Charles had shown himself a hypocrite who had broken
his trust. Oliver urged the Commons not to be afraid of dangers,
difficulties and the dissatisfaction of the people at large. If there was
'a lion in the way' they must overcome it. As he ended his speech,
he laid his hand on his sword. Immediately afterwards he wrote to
Colonel Hammond informing him of the vote and warning him of
the King's dealings and jugglings. The General Council of the Army
then agreed to accept the authority of a new Committee of Safety set
up by parliament of which Oliver became a leading member.

Under the impact of Charles I's tergiversations Oliver was becoming more and more dubious of the value of the monarchy as a sacro-
sanct institution. His attitude was more eclectic than ever. During a
conference held in his house in King Street, Westminster (where he
had moved from Drury Lane during the summer), Oliver refused to
commit himself in favour of monarchy, aristocracy or democracy,
'maintaining that any of them might be good in themselves, or for
us, according as providence shall direct us.' But in a speech in the
Commons in February 1648 he 'made a severe invective against
monarchical government.' That was no doubt inspired by his growing distrust of Charles I. Early in April he wrote to Hammond asking
him to ensure that Charles did not escape from Carisbrooke Castle.

By now it was clear that a second civil war was about to break out. In Essex and Kent, in Wales and Scotland, movements in support of Charles I were taking place. Although the Independent chaplains, whose influence on Oliver had been so strong, left the army at the beginning of the year, in early March William Dell and Hugh Peter turned up in Romford in Essex and tried to stem the Royalist reaction. Oliver was obliged to exert force to quell riots in London during April and he also aimed to unite Parliament by voting on the 28th of the month along with his more radical friend, Harry Vane, in favour of not altering the fundamental government by King, Lords and Commons. Two days later he was also attempting to create a united spirit in the army by pressing the Council of War to seek guidance through prayer. Five days later, under orders from General Fairfax, he led a military expedition into Wales. In London he had, under the influence of William Dell, been re-examining the bases of Independency. Hugh Peter accompanied him into Wales where he made himself useful by collecting artillery for the siege of Pembroke, whose governor had changed sides.

The second civil war was soon over. On 11 July, Pembroke surrendered and a month later Oliver met John Lambert in Leeds and planned the defeat of the Scottish Engagers and the northern Royalists. In one of his most brilliant campaigns he crushed his enemies in Lancashire and then marched into Scotland to establish order there. The only remaining centre of resistance in the north was at Pontefract Castle in Yorkshire. At the beginning of November, Oliver took personal charge of the siege.

While Oliver remained in the north Harry Vane and Henry Ireton had been politically active. Parliament decided to make a final effort to come to an agreement with Charles I. Vane was appointed one of the commissioners sent to negotiate with him at Newport in the Isle of Wight. Oliver wrote to Colonel Hammond, whom he addressed as 'dear Robin', asking him to warn Vane, whom he called 'my brother Heron', not to go too far in granting concessions, especially over religion. Harry Vane, like Oliver, soon concluded that Charles I was insincere. Since the second civil war began Oliver was convinced too that Charles was 'a man against whom the Lord hath witnessed.' But Henry Ireton now wanted immediate action. He demanded that the King, as 'the grand author of our troubles', together with his chief advisers, should be brought to justice for all the blood he had caused to flow. Ireton and the republican Ludlow were prepared forcibly to reconstitute the House of Commons if the majority insisted on continuing negotiations with the King. General Fairfax reluctantly agreed to extreme measures. He also dispatched one of his more radical colonels to replace Hammond as Charles's guardian on the Isle of Wight.

Oliver deliberately delayed in Yorkshire while he debated his own position or possibly the right tactics to pursue. He told Fairfax that his regimental officers were anxious to have impartial justice done to all offenders and he wrote to Hammond on 25 November that 'we in this northern army are in a waiting position desiring to see what the Lord would lead us into.' He confessed that it was difficult to interpret the providences of God, for they might be only 'fleshly reasonings'

Woodcut showing the abortive negotiations which took place at Newport in the Isle of Wight between Charles I and the parliamentary commissioners

Charles I: detail from the triple portrait by Anthony van Dyck. Van Dyck invariably flattered the King

sent to 'ensnare'. But the die had been cast. Before Oliver even wrote this last letter, Hammond was replaced, the Newport negotiations were abandoned, and the decision was taken in Whitehall to bring Charles to London to be put on trial for his war guilt.

On 6 December, Ireton and Ludlow carried out their proposed 'purge' of the House of Commons. The members who had favoured continuing the negotiations at Newport were expelled through the agency of Colonel Thomas Pride or voluntarily withdrew, leaving a 'rump' of some 150 members. Oliver arrived in London, having been ordered up by Fairfax, on the evening after Pride's Purge had taken place. He accepted that the Purge was necessary, although he evidently would have preferred the House of Commons to reconstitute itself. It is understandable that Oliver, who himself had been a member of parliament for twenty years, should have been anxious to arrange matters in a constitutional or legal way. One of the first things he did therefore on returning to London was to go down to Windsor to interview the first Duke of Hamilton, who had led the Scottish Engagers into England and had been taken a prisoner during the Preston campaign, in order to collect evidence against Charles I. Hamilton refused to betray the King and on the following day Oliver agreed to a resolution carried in the Council of Officers that the King, Hamilton and other principal Royalists should be speedily brought to justice. Yet he differed from his son-in-law, Ireton, in believing that

the other offenders should be put on trial before the King, presumably
in the hope that they would provide evidence against their master.
That, however, was a purely tactical consideration. No solid proof
exists for the suggestion that Oliver wanted to frighten the King
into unconditional surrender to extreme parliamentary terms. On
26 December Oliver told the House of Commons that he submitted
to providence and accepted that Charles must not merely be tried but
deposed.

Once Oliver made up his mind he hesitated no longer. He acted
along with Henry Ireton, Edward Whalley, Thomas Harrison and
some of the other army colonels, as one of the commissioners in the
High Court, set up by the remnants of the Commons to try the King.
But his friends, Harry Vane and Oliver St John, would not act and
nor would Fairfax, Skippon, Lambert, Fleetwood or Desborough.
Oliver, however, could count on the moral support of some of his
old friends, the army chaplains, including John Owen, Hugh Peter,
John Goodwin and others. Peter, preaching to the Commons on a
special fast day, said that its members could trust the army to lead them
out of 'Egyptian bondage' and to root up the monarchy.

The King refused to plead because he would not recognize the
jurisdiction of the court, set up by a truncated House of Commons.
Oliver attended all the sessions and agreed to the sentence of execution.
He energetically collected signatures for the death warrant. For it was
his belief that impartial justice had been done and a tyrant turned out.

OLIVARIVS CROMWELL EXERCITVVM ANGLIÆ
TENENS ET GVBERNATOR HIBERNIÆ OXO

REIPVBLICÆ DVX GENERALIS. LOCVM
NIENSIS ACADEMIÆ CANCELLARIVS

Oliver Cromwell never had the slightest doubt, after he had finally made up his mind at Christmas 1648, that the decision to put the King to death for war guilt was a right one. He told the General Council of Officers at Whitehall in March 1649: 'God hath brought the war to an issue and given you great fruit of that war, to wit: the execution of exemplary justice upon the prime leader of all this quarrel.' Then he prepared to carry out his responsibilities in the new Commonwealth government. In February he had been elected a member of the Council of State which was to be the executive branch of the republic; he was the only man who was a serving officer, a member of parliament and a regicide to be so elected. The Council of State met early in the morning or in the afternoon at hours which did not clash with the sitting of parliament. As Oliver also remained second in command of the army, from the outset he was overwhelmed with duties, though he managed to find time to negotiate the marriage of his son Richard to the girl he loved.

In most revolutions the victors include both moderates and extremists. Oliver remained a man of the middle; indeed he argued for the retention of the House of Lords, which was nevertheless abolished. There were few radicals in the Council of State; Henry Ireton, who had engaged in negotiations with the Levellers, was rejected by parliament for the Council of State, and so was Thomas Harrison, who had served under Ireton at the battle of Naseby and whose cavalry regiment had mutinied when the General Council of the Army refused in 1647 to accept the full programme of the Levellers.

The Levellers were extremely indignant over the new government: 'We were before ruled by King, Lords and Commons; now by a General, a Court Martial and House of Commons; and we pray what is the difference?' they asked. They thought that the country was under a more arbitrary monarchy then ever before and that 'fair blossoms of hopeful liberty' had ripened into 'bitter fruit'. Their leader, John Lilburne, had promptly produced pamphlets entitled *England's New Chains Discovered* and *England's New Chains Part II*. Leveller propaganda against the new regime permeated the rank and file of the army. Cromwell was subjected to harsh reproaches. After eight troopers were court-martialled and five of them cashiered for having approved the arguments in Lilburne's pamphlets, yet another pamphlet appeared, in which John Lilburne probably had a hand, though it was attributed to the five cashiered troopers: 'You shall scarce speak to Cromwell about anything but he will lay his hand on his breast, elevate his eyes, and call God to record; he will weep, howl and repent, even while he doth smite you under the fifth rib.'

The relations between Oliver and John Lilburne were in fact ambivalent: it was a strong love-hate relationship. When John Lilburne was only eighteen he had been whipped through the

(*Opposite*) equestrian portrait of Cromwell: a Dutch engraving which is hardly a good likeness

67

AN IMPEACHMENT
OF
HIGH TREASON
AGAINST

Oliver Cromwel, and his Son in Law *Henry Ireton* Efquires, late Members of the late forcibly diffolved Houfe of Commons, prefented to publique view ; by *Lieutenant Colonel Iohn Lilburn* clofe Prifoner in the Tower of London, for his real, true and zealous affections to the Liberties of his native Country.

In which following Difcourfe or Impeachment, he engageth upon his life, either upon the principles of Law (*by way of indiEtment, the only and alone legall way of all tryals in England*) or upon the principles of Parliaments ancient proceedings, or upon the principles of reafon (*by pretence of which alone, they lately took away the Kings life*) before a legal Magiftracy, when there fhal be one again in England (*which now in the leaft there is not*) to prove the faid *Oliver Cromwel* guilty of the higheft Treafon that ever was acted in England, and more deferving punifhment and death

---

Title-page of one of John Lilburne's pamphlets directed against Cromwell and Ireton after the execution of King Charles I in 1649

streets of London and thrown into the Fleet prison for distributing subversive literature aimed against the bishops. One of the first things that Oliver did after he was elected to the Long Parliament had been to demand Lilburne's release. According to another member of that parliament, Oliver had 'aggravated the imprisonment of this man . . . unto that height that one would have believed the very Government itself had been in great danger by it.' John Lilburne was soon released and later rose to the rank of lieutenant-colonel in the Earl of Manchester's army, fighting on the wing commanded by Oliver at the battle of Marston Moor. John at that time regarded Oliver as his 'most intimate and familiar bosom friend' and backed his accusation of dilatoriness against Manchester. Partly because of further accusations against Manchester, Lilburne had been put into Newgate prison by the House of Lords for contempt and later in 1646 was transferred to the Tower of London. Here, as has been noted, Oliver visited him during the following year and tried to persuade him not to stir up trouble in the army at a critical time. John refused; nevertheless Oliver did his utmost to procure his release on bail and when the second civil war began, John, at last completely freed from the Tower, promised Oliver that if he followed 'the righteous ways of truth and justice' he would shed the last drop of his heart's blood for him. This despite the accusation put out by the Levellers that Oliver had been intriguing with Charles I and had been promised an earl-

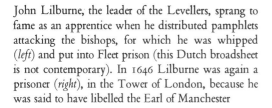

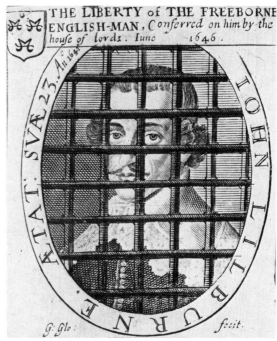

THE LIBERTY of THE FREEBORNE ENGLISH-MAN, *Conferred on him by the house of lords: June* 1646.

Meester Lilburn achter een kar gegeeselt.
Mr. Lilburne whipt after the Cart's tayle.

John Lilburne, the leader of the Levellers, sprang to fame as an apprentice when he distributed pamphlets attacking the bishops, for which he was whipped (*left*) and put into Fleet prison (this Dutch broadsheet is not contemporary). In 1646 Lilburne was again a prisoner (*right*), in the Tower of London, because he was said to have libelled the Earl of Manchester

dom. In fact Oliver was in agreement with many of the Leveller ideas, such as the need for the reform of the law, for constitutional revision and for religious toleration.

But what Oliver as a military commander would not stand for was the subversion of the army. That was why in May 1649 he agreed to the arrest of Lilburne and other Leveller leaders on suspicion of treason: 'You have no other way to deal with these men,' he told the Council of State, 'but to break them or they will break you.' So once again John Lilburne was put back in the Tower, but in July he was released on bail out of compassion for his wife and children who were all struck down by smallpox. Soon after he procured this release (two of his sons died), John Lilburne published *An Impeachment of Treason against Oliver Cromwell and his Son-in-Law Henry Ireton* in which he accused Oliver, a little fantastically, of planning to become another Cardinal Wolsey. Put back in prison and later committed for trial, Lilburne was acquitted by a London jury of being guilty of treason through acts of subversion. Less than a year afterwards Lilburne was to be found accompanying Oliver Cromwell up the Great North Road on his way to Scotland: the two men embraced each other as they said goodbye. Just before his death in 1657 John Lilburne was converted to the Quaker faith. Oliver, by then Lord Protector, promptly provided a pension and a home for Lilburne's widow.

But to return to 1649. As a member of the Council of State, Oliver was entitled to advise the arrest of John Lilburne for security reasons, yet he was not the commander-in-chief who was responsible for carrying out such duties. Although General Fairfax had disapproved of the trial of Charles I for his life, and his wife, Anne, Lady Fairfax, had screamed from the public gallery during the trial that Oliver Cromwell was a traitor, the two men remained on terms of friendship and mutual respect all their lives. After all, few men can control the behaviour of their wives. Oliver persuaded Fairfax to join the Council of State without requiring him to take any oath approving the King's execution. On 31 March, Fairfax was appointed by parliament commander-in-chief of all the forces of the Commonwealth of England. It was Fairfax, above all, who insisted on maintaining strict discipline in the army. On the other hand, when Edward Whalley suppressed a mutiny in his regiment which took place in the City of London, it was Oliver who pleaded for mercy and Fairfax who required that the ringleader should be executed. Equally it was under Fairfax's orders that mutineers in one of the cavalry regiments were rounded up at Burford in Oxfordshire. Three hundred and forty of them were taken prisoner and three of them shot by order of Fairfax. After the execution Oliver addressed the remaining mutineers and stressed Fairfax's mercy in pardoning all but three of them, allowing the rest to go home.

One of the biggest threats to the English Commonwealth came from Ireland, where the Marquis of Ormonde, a devoted servant of the late King, had succeeded in building up an alliance between the native Irish and the English settlers who were Royalists and even the Presbyterian Scots who dwelt in Ulster. Thus for a time he dominated the island and England's left flank was menaced. If Ormonde could unite Ireland, he might even be able to invade England in the name of King Charles II. The Council of State was fully conscious of the danger and as early as the middle of March 1649 had nominated Oliver as commander-in-chief of an expeditionary army to reinforce the troops already there; later parliament also appointed him Lord-Lieutenant of Ireland. As usual, Oliver hesitated whether to accept the post, abandoning the key position he held in London. But by the end of March he was convinced where his duty lay: 'Let us go,' he said, 'if God go.'

But he laid down conditions. He insisted that he needed five cavalry regiments, six infantry regiments and 1,200 dragoons and that in view of the temper of the army his men should be given their arrears of pay and an advance for three months. Adequate supplies of food, munitions and clothing were also required by him plus £100,000 in cash. His task of preparing for the expedition was by no means easy. The army had been unruly and the Levellers had been advocating

Dr John Owen (*left*), whom Cromwell appointed Vice-Chancellor of Oxford University. He was at one time an army chaplain and he influenced Cromwell's thinking about the organization of a State Church

Lieutenant-General George Monck. Cromwell, impressed by Monck's services in Ireland, put him in command of a regiment during the Scottish campaign of 1650–51. Later Monck became the military governor of Scotland and remained steadfastly loyal to Oliver

rather impractical schemes for a free and independent Ireland. The names of the regiments to go to Ireland were chosen by lot, a small child pulling the names out of a hat. Men in these regiments who did not want to serve there were allowed to leave the army. Oliver was given his son-in-law, Ireton, who had refused to have anything to do with the suppression of the Levellers, as his second in command. Although Lambert's regiment was one of those selected, John Lambert himself did not accompany Oliver. For his chaplain Oliver chose Dr John Owen, a prolific theologian who repeatedly insisted that Christ died for the Elect only, in preference to Hugh Peter, who was a bit of a buffoon and a busy-body, though he loved Oliver dearly, and went with him to Milford Haven, the port of embarkation, where he acted as a kind of muster master. Owen was a cut above Peter. Educated at Queen's College, Oxford, which he entered at the age of twelve, he had moved from Presbyterianism to Independency; selected as chaplain to the Council of State, he had preached before parliament on the day after Charles I's execution. The sermon was expanded into a pamphlet which surely appealed to Oliver, *A Discourse about Toleration and the Duty of the Civil Magistrate*. But Owen, like Peter, belonged to the Church Militant. Six years later he was to be seen riding at the head of a troop of horse with his sword and pistol in hand ready to put down a Royalist rising. Oliver's other great friend, William Dell, had been appointed, probably through Oliver's influence, Master of the College of Gonville and Caius at Cambridge.

Oliver finally left Whitehall on 10 July, accompanied by Ireton, and drove to Bristol, from which he refused to stir until he was assured

The Irish campaign 1649–50

that all the supplies and money he had been promised had arrived. His wife and eldest son came to say goodbye to him. On the eve of his departure from Milford Haven he met a man who was to play an important part in his life: this was George Monck, a dedicated professional officer who had first served the King but then had been given a command in Ulster by parliament. Monck had felt obliged to sign an armistice with Owen Roe O'Neill, a guerrilla warrior and the leader of the native Irish in Ulster, in order to prevent Ormonde's troops from over-running the country. Monck told Oliver he had no alternative to signing the armistice. The parliament at Westminster was indignant that Monck had shaken hands with 'a popish monster' and dismissed him, but Oliver evidently recognized the military necessity of his decision and later was to recompense him when it looked as if Monck's military career was over.

As he left England in August 1649 Oliver's last thoughts were with his eldest son and new daughter-in-law. He wrote a letter to Richard's father-in-law, which he gave Richard to take to him. It said:

I have committed my son to you; pray give him advice. I envy him not his contents; but I fear he should be swallowed up of them. I would have him mind and understand business, read a little history, study the mathematics and cosmography: these are good with subordination to the things of God. Better than idleness or mere outward worldly contents. These fit for *public service, for which a man is born.* . . .

Before he actually sailed, Oliver learned the good news that Ormonde's army had been completely defeated outside Dublin by Major-General Michael Jones, who had been reinforced by two regiments sent in advance by Cromwell. The victory simplified Oliver's task in Ireland and he rewarded Jones by appointing him as second in command instead of Ireton. But a few months later Jones died and Ireton succeeded him. Oliver also took with him to Ireland a former Royalist (like Monck) in Roger Boyle, Lord Broghill, the son of the Earl of Cork, whom he appointed Master of Ordnance. 'To him was due in no small measure the success of the Irish expedition, and he became not only one of Cromwell's ablest supporters but one of his closest friends.' (Abbott.) As in his younger days, Oliver was indifferent to his soldiers' religious and political affiliations; if they would serve the cause faithfully, that was enough.

Oliver's campaign in Ireland was quick, ruthless and effective. By the time he took up winter quarters at the end of 1649 almost the whole coastline was in English hands. Oliver's decision soon after his arrival to put the garrison of Drogheda to the sword when the defenders refused to surrender, even after breaches had been blown in the walls, spread terror in Irish hearts. Oliver believed that the 'justice done upon "these barbarous wretches" would tend to prevent the effusion of blood for the future, which are the satisfactory grounds

Drogheda, captured by Cromwell in 1649 after the garrison had refused to surrender on terms; most but not all of the garrison was put to the sword

for such actions, *which cannot otherwise but work remorse and regret.*' Militarily speaking, Oliver's case was impregnable, but of course he laid the responsibility not upon himself but upon God.

Oliver's difficulties in Ireland consisted chiefly of appalling weather and heavy medical casualties. His men were decimated by malaria and dysentery, and Oliver himself seems to have first contracted there the malaria from which he was ultimately to die. But he revealed what many believe to be the highest qualities of generalship in keeping open good communications to furnish his army with food and sup/plies and by making full use of sea power. In January 1650 he was recalled to England and in May he finally handed over his command to Henry Ireton as his Lord Deputy. Ireton largely completed Crom/well's conquest, but in November 1651 he caught cold and died of pneumonia. Oliver's able second son, Henry, was with Ireton at the last. Some contemporaries were of the opinion that Ireton, who had a superb intellect, was Oliver's mentor on political questions. It was said that 'Cromwell only shot the bolts that were hammered in Ireton's forge.' Henry Ireton preceded his father/in/law in formulating a balanced constitution and was far more sympathetic to the ideals of the Levellers than Oliver ever was. What is certain is that no younger man ever stood so close to Oliver as Henry Ireton did.

Oliver crossed the Irish Channel towards the end of May; he was as seasick coming back as he had been on the journey out. His reception at Windsor by leading members of the Council of State and parliament was a warm one and he was also greeted by his wife who had come to meet him. When he reached London he re/established friendly rela/tions with the Lord General Fairfax and attended meetings of the Council of State. The reason for his recall from Ireland was that the Council of State was perturbed by events in Scotland. At the begin/ning of May the youthful Charles II had come to terms with the Scottish Covenanters who negotiated with him in Holland, and he was now preparing to sail across the North Sea to be crowned King of the Scots. The original intention in London was to send Cromwell to lead an expedition against the Scots while Fairfax remained behind to provide for the security of England. But parliament over/ruled the Council of State and decided that both Fairfax and Cromwell should go to Scotland, while the fanatical Puritan, Major/General Thomas Harrison, should take charge in England.

At first both Fairfax and Cromwell agreed to go. But when Fairfax discovered that the intention was to invade Scotland he withdrew his consent. He maintained that such a move was contrary to the Solemn League and Covenant, which all English officers had accepted, and moreover he saw no justification for a preventive war. Oliver did his utmost to induce Fairfax to change his mind. Mrs Lucy Hutchinson, who was no admirer of Cromwell, wrote in her memoirs that no one

The following text appears within the caricature illustration:

THE SCOTS HOLDING THEIR YOVNG KINGES NOSE TO Y GRINSTO

Come to the Grinstone Charles tis now to late:
To Recolect tis presbiterian fate.

You, Couinant pretenders must Sheer
The Subiect of your Trudgie Comedie.

Jockie

Scoope Charles

A caricature of the Scots holding Charles II's nose to the grindstone in 1650: a broadsheet dated 1651

at the time doubted Oliver's sincerity and that in his attempt to persuade Fairfax he 'laboured it almost all the night with earnest endeavours.' Fairfax could not be moved and on 26 June Oliver was appointed captain-general in his place. In fact Fairfax was right; the Scots had at that time not the slightest intention of invading England in the name of Charles II. The truth too was that Fairfax, a modest and cultured man, and his assertive wife found the republic distasteful and retired to the quiet of the Yorkshire countryside to await the return of the monarchy.

Oliver did not hesitate for a moment. John Lambert was sent ahead to Doncaster to prepare for the concentration of the invasion force. Charles Fleetwood, an agreeable if weak-minded officer of about Lambert's age, was appointed lieutenant-general of the cavalry and Oliver brought George Monck out of his retirement in Devonshire to be a supernumerary colonel for whom in due course he provided a regiment. Oliver made Edward Whalley his commissary-general (second in command of the cavalry) and John Lilburne's brother Robert took command of one of the cavalry regiments. John Lambert was to take charge of the infantry. The chaplains who served with the expedition included John Owen and Joseph Cargill, both Independents; Hugh Peter, who was growing old, remained behind as chaplain to the Council of State.

The layout of the English army at the battle of Dunbar, fought on 3 September 1650. In the right-hand bottom corner the town and Cromwell's base camp are to be seen. The Parliamentarian army was supplied from the sea and the wounded evacuated by sea. In the left-hand top corner is the cottage which Cromwell's men occupied as an advanced outpost

Oliver regarded the Scots in quite a different light from the Irish. He thought the Irish were barbarians and tried to stop them celebrating the 'popish Mass'. But the Scots, after all, were fellow Puritans and he hoped to win them over with fair words. Hence the importance of his chaplains. As he wrote later to the Council of State: 'Since we came to Scotland, it hath been our desire and longing to have

Medal commemorating the battle of
Dunbar: the portrait was done from
life by Thomas Simon

Woodcut from a ballad on the
battle of Dunbar

avoided blood in this business, by reason that God hath a people
here fearing His name, though deceived.' The chaplains were set to
work composing appeals to the 'Saints' of Scotland. An animated, if
not altogether amicable, correspondence ensued. Both contestants
were convinced that they had God on their side. Oliver wrote to the
General Assembly of the Kirk of Scotland: 'I beseech you, in the

bowels of Christ, think it possible that you may be mistaken'; and he told them that 'there may be a covenant with death and hell.'

However, in the end the war had to be fought out. Although the English army was cornered by the Scots at Dunbar, east of Edinburgh, Oliver, acting on the advice of Lambert and Monck, decided on a dawn attack after a wet night which had concealed the movements of his troops. The Scots, who outnumbered the English by two to one, were decisively defeated. After the victory on 3 September 1650 Oliver wrote to his wife to tell her of 'the exceeding mercy' which had upheld his 'weak faith'. He went on: 'thou art dearer to me than any creature'; he confessed: 'I grow an old man'; and he asked her to apply to Harry Vane for the details of the late success.

In spite of this defeat and the English occupation of Edinburgh, the Scots did not surrender. Commanded by the experienced David Leslie and inspired by the youthful Charles II, they defied Cromwell along the line of the river Forth. During the spring of 1651 Oliver was taken seriously ill. It was not until July that he worked out a plan, with the active assistance of John Lambert, to manœuvre the Scots out of their strong position. He sent Lambert across the Forth to menace the Scots' rear and after Lambert had defeated the Scottish detachment sent against him, Oliver followed him up with the bulk of his army. That left the road to England open. At the end of July, Charles II led an army, composed mainly of Scots, from Stirling to Carlisle and aimed to arouse Lancashire and Wales against the Commonwealth government.

A seventeenth-century painting of Stirling, to which General David Leslie retreated after his defeat by Cromwell at Dunbar

Castrum puellarum

Oliver was not taken by surprise. He sent Lambert with a cavalry force after Charles and called up Major-General Harrison who was stationed at Newcastle-upon-Tyne to join Lambert. Oliver himself came behind with the infantry. Charles Fleetwood, who had returned to London six months after the battle of Dunbar and had raised a fresh army, marched to the Midlands to meet them. By the beginning of September, Charles II and his army were trapped and surrounded by a much superior force in the town of Worcester. The result of the battle was predictable. Afterwards Oliver wrote to the Speaker: 'It is, for aught I know, a crowning mercy,' and praised its dimensions. But he owed much to Lambert and Harrison, Fleetwood and Monck (whom he left behind to hold Scotland) and the other officers of his well-trained armies. He was, it is true, their leader; but they made up his world and as events were to prove, he was also their servant.

Oliver had the highest hopes in the Commonwealth, which he had so successfully defended against its enemies. His admirer, John Milton, the poet who was made Latin Secretary to the Council of State, had envisaged a 'noble and puissant nation rousing herself like a strong man after sleep, and shaking her invincible locks.' Following his victory at Dunbar, Oliver had urged the Speaker of parliament:

Disown yourselves, but own your authority, and improve it to curb the proud and insolent, such as would disturb the tranquillity of England, though under what specious pretexts soever; relieve the oppressed, hear the groans of poor prisoners in England; be pleased to reform the abuses of all professions; and if there be anyone that makes many poor to make a few rich, that suits not a Commonwealth.

A contemporary map of Edinburgh, which was occupied by Cromwell's army after Dunbar

(*Overleaf*) 'An exact ground-plot of the City of Worcester as it stood fortified' on 3 September 1651

79

An exact Ground-Plot of ỹ C
WORCESTE
as it stood fortifyd, 3. Sept.
Sold by Anne Seile neere St. Dunstans Church in Fle

The way to London

1	The Cathedral, or Colledge Church	15	Castle Gate
2	St. Peters Church	16	Colledge Gate
3	St. Andrews Church	17	Sudbury Gate
4	St. Martins Church	18	St. Martins Gate
5	St. Nicholas Church	19	Fore-Gate
6	St. Clements Church	20	Friers Gate
7	St. Albans Church	21	Frog-Gate
8	St. Helens Church	22	High-Streete
9	St. Swithins Church	23	Friers-Streete
10	St. Iohns	24	Pitch-croft
11	All Sts. Church	25	Bridge over Severn
12	The Fort Royal	26	The Water house
13	Castle hill	27	The Key
14	Bishops Palace		

But it was not long after he returned to London that Oliver and his army felt disappointed with the activities of the Rump Parliament. The Commonwealth had been committed to a naval war against the Dutch which was expensive and distasteful to the army. At home, some attempts had been made to plan the reform of the law, to assist the poor and to promote religious liberty. Acts against adultery, swearing and blasphemy had been passed. But other reforms were paralysed by inertia. Dr John Owen's carefully thought-out scheme for settling ecclesiastical questions was not accepted. In August 1652 a petition from the army, though modified by Cromwell, demanded swift and radical reforms. The opinion spread – rightly or wrongly – that many members of parliament were selfish and corrupt and that they were 'more protective of the rich and powerful than the poor and oppressed.' (Underdown.) Another modern historian has written: 'The Rump was an oligarchy with no positive policy except that of self-interest.' (George Yule.)

Towards the end of the year Oliver told Bulstrode Whitelocke, another member of parliament: 'Really their pride and ambition and self-seeking ingrossing all places of honour and profit to themselves and their friends and their daily breaking forth into new and violent ... factions, their delay of business and designs to perpetuate themselves ... do give too much ground for people to open their mouths against them. . . .' Nevertheless, for months Oliver, who was twice returned at the top of the poll for membership of the Council of State, tried to restrain the army extremists from moving against parliament. He would have preferred that a change of government should be brought about amicably and legally. Discussions were arranged under Oliver's auspices outside the House of Parliament on how to replace the rule of the Rump by means of an agreed constitutional settlement. Major-General Lambert wanted a small committee to be appointed to draft a new constitution; Major-General Harrison advocated government by 'Saints' until Jesus Christ should come back to rule the earth. So Oliver was under severe pressures from his officers and army. But all of them were determined that parliament should dissolve and allow time for a fresh start.

The army leaders thus sought for an immediate and radical change. The corrupt and self-seeking Rumpers, they believed, should be replaced by men of integrity and good will. Oliver himself was to say: 'We desired that they should devolve the trust to persons of honour and integrity that were well known, men well affected to religion and the interest of the nation.'

In April 1653 it was reported that 'the General sticks close to the House', and after a month's absence he reappeared in parliament to plead for its immediate dissolution of its own accord. On the evening of 19 April a number of officers and members of parliament met in

The Great Seal of the
Commonwealth, showing the
House of Parliament in 1651

Cromwell's lodgings and seem to have agreed to consider setting up
an interim committee of council to undertake arrangements for calling
a new parliament in place of the Rump. No doubt a misunderstand‚
ing arose over exactly what had been agreed. At any rate when the
next day the Rump Parliament began discussing a Bill setting out
detailed proposals for dissolution and the election of a new parliament,
to which it would transfer its powers, Oliver lost his temper. Evi‚
dently he thought that the Rump intended to perpetuate itself in
defiance of the wishes of the army. He observed, after a speech which
had begun mildly enough, that the members of parliament included
drunkards and 'whoremasters', corrupt and unjust men, and some
who had broken their word. He was particularly severe on Harry
Vane, a man whom he had once called brother and with whom he
had been on terms of intimacy. At last Oliver said: 'Come, come, I
will put an end to your prating.' He called in two files of musketeers
and ordered them to clear the House. Then he looked at the Mace,
the symbol of the Speaker's authority: 'What shall we do with this
bauble?' he exclaimed: 'Here, take it away.'

A Dutch print giving an
imaginative picture of Oliver
Cromwell (with stick) dissolving
the Rump Parliament

THIS HOVSE IS TO LETE

This is an Oule.

The Rump had failed to complete religious, social and political reforms largely because its methods of governing were unwieldy, its members divided and vested interests obstructive. It had antagonized the army and some of its members were corrupt. Even before Oliver suddenly dissolved it, he had clearly made up his mind to replace it with those whom he called 'men of proved integrity': he sought for a rule by 'Saints'. Completely rejecting the idea of setting himself up as a dictator, he summoned an Assembly of Saints, nominated by the Council of the Army. In welcoming this nominated assembly of 140 members, who first met in May 1653, Oliver greeted it with two quotations from the Old Testament: 'This people, saith God, I have formed for myself, that they may show forth my praise', and 'He that ruleth over men must be just, ruling in the fear of God.' He added that he wished all 'were fit to be called', but alas it was not so.

The 'Saints', among whom were sober merchants, lesser gentry and schoolmasters, laboured to fashion a Brave New World. They rapidly pushed through reforms. Maybe they drove too fast and furiously. Certainly they managed to alienate many classes in the community. They annoyed Cromwell by pushing on with the Anglo-Dutch war which he did not like and they failed to consult him. They upset property-owners by attacking property rights. They disturbed Dr Owen and the more intelligent ecclesiastical reformers by promoting a kind of legalized spiritual anarchy. They even angered the Levellers by once more throwing John Lilburne into prison.

So – like the Rump Parliament – the Assembly of Saints achieved little or nothing permanent. Their creator, Oliver Cromwell, afterwards thought that they exemplified his own 'weakness and folly'. Indeed he later criticized his army officers for even nominating such an assembly. 'What did the Convention of *your* choosing?' he asked four years later. 'Fly at liberty and property, insomuch as if one man had twelve cows, they held another that wanted cows ought to share

A naval engagement during the Dutch war, said to have taken place near Leghorn. Oliver brought this war to an end soon after he became Protector

In this Dutch print of negotiations for a Dutch offer of peace in 1653 Cromwell is represented rejecting the offer, though in reality he was opposed to pushing on with the war

with his neighbour.' The radical members looked for guidance not to Oliver but to Thomas Harrison, who (like Lambert and Monck) was a member of the Assembly, and to Harrison's friends, the Fifth Monarchy preachers, who believed in the imminent arrival of Christ on earth. Who would you have rule you, these preachers asked, Oliver Cromwell or Jesus Christ?

The Assembly of Saints was destroyed by a *coup d'état* organized mainly by John Lambert. One December morning in 1653 the moderates in the Assembly got up very early and handed their power back to the Captain-General who had originally bestowed it upon them. A new constitution (known as the Instrument of Government) was drawn up naming Oliver Cromwell as Lord Protector of the Commonwealth. Major-General Thomas Harrison, the architect of the Assembly of Saints, would not acknowledge the Protectorate and refused all posts offered him. He preferred to retire to his home in Newcastle-under-Lyme, which he had inherited from his father, the butcher, who had been four times mayor. John Lambert, the maker of the third revolution, became Cromwell's 'vice-regent'.

THE LORD PROTECTOR   Cromwell's seal; the Protectorate seal; Cromwell's Sword of State; and a proclamation declaring Cromwell Lord Protector on 16 December 1653

BY THE COVNCIL.

WHEREAS the late Parliament dissolving themselves, and resigning their Powers and Authorities, The Government of the Commonwealth of England, Scotland, and Ireland, by a LORD PROTECTOR, and Successive Triennial Parliaments, is now established; And Whereas OLIVER CROMWELL, Captain-General of all the Forces of this Commonwealth, is declared LORD PROTECTOR of the said Nations, and hath accepted thereof: We have therefore thought it necessary (as we hereby do) to make publication of the Premisses, and strictly to Charge and Command all and every person and persons, of what Quality and Condition soever, in any of the said three Nations, to take notice hereof and to conform and submit themselves to the Government so established. And all Sheriffs, Maiors, Bayliffs, and other Publick Ministers, and Officers, whom this may concern, are required to cause this PROCLAMATION to be forthwith published in their respective Counties, Cities, Corporations, and Market-Towns, To the end none may have Cause to pretend ignorance in this behalf.
Given at White-Hall this sixteenth day of December, 1653.

(Opposite) The Embleme of Englands Distractions. In this allegorical representation Cromwell is depicted trampling monstrous Faction and Error and the Whore of Babylon underfoot

The EMBLEME
of ENGLANDS Distractions
As also of her attained, and further
expected Freedome, & Happines
Per H.M.
1658

Anthony Ashley Cooper (later the first Earl of Shaftesbury) who served in Cromwell's Council of State

John Milton, the Latin Secretary of the Council of State. Milton wrote two celebrated sonnets about Cromwell, but appears to have disapproved of the Protectorate

Oliver always believed that the Protectorate was equitable and far from arbitrary. 'I was a child in swaddling clothes,' he said in later life, and emphasized that he could 'do nothing but in ordination with the Council.' The nine months that followed its establishment was the most constructive period in his life. He had an able group of men to work with him in his government. Besides the hard-headed Lambert, he had a highly capable administrator in his Secretary of State, John Thurloe, who was in the prime of his life, and managed to combine the duties of home secretary, foreign minister and director of the intelligence service. Sir Gilbert Pickering, like Thurloe a devoted friend of Oliver, looked after the foreign ambassadors and the necessary ceremonies at Court. Matthew Hale, a future Lord Chief Justice, advised Oliver on law reform; he also had the help of Anthony Ashley Cooper, a future Lord Chancellor, and of the omnipresent Hugh Peter who fancied he was knowledgeable about Dutch law.

To lovers of English literature it would be of interest to know precisely what part the great poet John Milton played in the world of Oliver Cromwell. Unhappily the information available is limited and even contradictory. 'When Oliver ascended the throne,' wrote Anthony Wood, an Oxford antiquary, 'he [Milton] became the Latin Secretary and proved to be very serviceable when employed in business of weight and moment, and did great matters to obtain a name and wealth.' But that is almost totally untrue. Milton was appointed Latin Secretary to the Commonwealth Council of State soon after Charles I's execution and not by the influence of Cromwell. Oliver had tried to persuade the lawyer, John Selden, to answer the book *Eikon Basilike*, 'the Portraiture of his Sacred Majesty in his Solitudes and Sufferings', which was supposed to have been written by the martyred monarch himself and was widely circulated. Milton then undertook the task and later wrote two other books, *The Defence of the People of England* (1651) and *The Second Defence* (1654) on behalf of the Commonwealth. Labouring at these books, he can scarcely have been overwhelmed by his duties as Latin Secretary, which was in any case a post of minor importance. Occasionally he attended meetings of the Council of State, mostly when Oliver was away fighting in Ireland and Scotland, but he was no longer required to be present after he went completely blind at the end of 1651.

Unquestionably Milton was a devoted admirer of Cromwell. In 1652 he wrote the famous sonnet in which he addressed Oliver as 'our chief of men' and told him that 'peace hath her victories no less renowned than war.' He approved of Pride's Purge, of Oliver's dissolution of the Rump Parliament and of the closure of the Assembly of Saints: 'they meet but do nothing,' he wrote, 'and have wearied themselves with their mutual dissensions and fully exposed their incapacity to the observations of the country. . . .' But Milton was disappointed that Oliver did not favour the separation of Church and State; and he warned him against autocracy:

But if you who have hitherto been the patron and tutelary genius of liberty, if you who are exceeded by no one in justice, in piety and goodness, should hereafter invade that liberty, which you have defended, your conduct must be fatally operative, not only against the cause of liberty but of the general interests of piety and virtue. Your integrity and virtue will appear to have evaporated, your faith in religion to have been small.

Oliver presumably was not unappreciative of his candid admirer (who had given him a copy of the sonnet) for he retained Milton in the post of Latin Secretary in an honorific capacity but at a salary of £200 a year for life after he went blind, while first Philip Meadows and then another poet, Andrew Marvell, did such work as was necessary. After Oliver's death Milton surprisingly wrote pamphlets condemning government by a single person and described the Protectorate as 'a short but scandalous night of interruption.' So Milton's political attitude was strangely inconsistent. It may well be that, like other men of his time, he trusted Cromwell not to abuse his position but had no faith in Cromwell's ambitious generals, particularly John Lambert.

John Thurloe, Cromwell's Secretary of State

In general the English people wanted peace and stability after the long civil wars. The record of the Protectorate's administrative deeds, carried out with the advice and support of the Council of State, is impressive. Most of the domestic questions, the solution of which had been attempted but not settled during the four and a half years since the death of Charles I, were at last put in order. The Church was placed on a sound footing by the appointment of a committee of 'triers' to approve the choice of ministers in the parishes, a committee which included Oliver's favourite chaplains, like Dr John Owen, Thomas Goodwin, Hugh Peter and Peter Sterry. Other committees were set up throughout the country to report on and, if necessary, to eject unsatisfactory or 'scandalous' ministers. These committees consisted of laymen whom Oliver trusted: for example, a committee-man in the West Riding of Yorkshire was Lord Fairfax. Ordinances were enacted to speed up justice, to widen the scope of assize judges, and to reform the Court of Chancery. Several measures were introduced to improve the lot of poor creditors thrust into prison for small debts. The chaotic conditions of the public finances, which had prevailed under the Rump, was straightened out and a centralized Treasury re-established. Cock-fighting and duelling were forbidden as well as drunkenness and swearing among the customs officers. The Post Office was reorganized and orders given that the highways should be repaired.

(*Above*) title-page of an ordinance of 1654 prohibiting cock-fighting. (*Below*) engraved title-page for *Catch that Catch Can* or a *Choice Collection of Catches etc* (1652), one of many light music books published in the period. Cromwell was very fond of music himself

(*Right*) an imaginative Dutch painting of a company of Puritans with Richard Cromwell shaking hands with a Dutch visitor (at door) accompanied by Dr John Owen

(*Left*) Charles Fleetwood, the second husband of Oliver's eldest daughter, Bridget. For a time he was Lord Deputy in Ireland, until replaced by Henry Cromwell. This miniature (*right*) is said to be of Henry, Oliver's second son, who survived him

Oliver was equally energetic in foreign affairs. Arrangements were completed in accordance with the terms of the Instrument of Government to hold elections in Scotland and Ireland so that both countries should have spokesmen at Westminster. Later an ordinance of union with Scotland was passed, while George Monck, who, being an artillery expert, had proved himself a good admiral in the Dutch war, was sent back to restore order and suppress unrest in Scotland. Charles Fleetwood, who had in 1652 married Ireton's widow, Oliver's eldest daughter, was appointed Lord Deputy in Ireland. A rather ineffective Puritan with republican sympathies, he did not prove a wise choice and in 1655 was replaced by Oliver's son Henry. Finally a continued effort was made to spread the Gospel to the more primitive parts of Wales. The Committee for the Propagation of the Gospel there, which was encouraged by Cromwell, became 'the real government of Wales'.

Abroad, Oliver brought to an end the naval war with the Dutch on excellent terms for England, though not hitting the Dutch unduly harshly; treaties were concluded with Sweden and Denmark and treaties of commerce negotiated with Portugal and France. Robert Blake, a famous admiral who is sometimes described as a dyed-in-the-wool republican but was in fact a loyal officer on cordial terms with Oliver, protected English ships trading in the Mediterranean. Oliver's Council was divided over whether an alliance should be concluded with either of the warring powers of France and Spain. For

Medal commemorating the ending
of the Anglo-Dutch war in 1654

example, Pickering was for France, Lambert for Spain. In the end
Oliver took what proved to be a decisive step when he organized an
amphibious expedition to sail across the Atlantic to seize one of the
Spanish West Indian islands; war with Spain was to begin late in
1655, and in 1656 an offensive treaty was concluded with France.

When Oliver met his first parliament in September 1654 – freely
elected in England and with members from Scotland and Ireland –
he justified the establishment of the Protectorate as having procured
'healing and settling' at home and peace and security abroad. He
asked that the ordinances which comprised his domestic policy should
be confirmed; and he concluded a well-arranged and eloquent
speech by telling members of parliament that they had 'great works'
upon their hands. It was, he said, 'one of the great ends of calling this
Parliament that this Ship of the Commonwealth may be brought
into a safe harbour; which, I assure you, it will not well be without
your counsel and advice.'

Oliver had good reason to hope that the 'freely elected' parliament
would co-operate with him in fashioning a peaceable Commonwealth.
The radical members of the Assembly of Saints were not elected to
it; Harry Vane, though offered a seat in the Assembly of Saints,
temporarily retired from political life and was absorbed in writing
cloudy religious treatises. Some of the more extreme republicans had
been deliberately prevented from entering parliament and although a
republican group of eighty headed by Arthur Haselrig, Thomas Scot

and John Bradshaw secured election, they were outnumbered by the Court group. But Oliver and his Council of State lacked an effective and dynamic leader in the House; the nearest to one perhaps was Anthony Ashley Cooper, a member of the lesser gentry of Dorset, but he had to contend with Haselrig and Scot who showed themselves to be persuasive orators and astute politicians. They argued that they were under no obligation to accept the Instrument of Government, but set about drawing up a new constitution in which Cromwell was at most to be a figurehead.

Oliver was perturbed lest such undermining of the Protectorate should produce disorder and dissension throughout the country. Thomas Harrison was stirring up unrest from his home in the north and republican conspirators were known to be plotting in London taverns. Oliver decided on drastic action. On 12 September he surrounded the House of Parliament with guards and delivered a long speech to the members. First he offered 'a cloud of witnesses' to prove that he had been called to his office not merely by God but by the whole nation. Though he reiterated that he regarded the members as constituting a free parliament, there must, he insisted, be 'a reciprocity', in other words they must acknowledge him as their chief executive officer. They must also, he affirmed, accept four fundamental principles: these were government by a single person and parliament, the division of control over the military forces of the nation between him and them, the limitation of the time for which parliament might sit, and 'liberty of conscience'. Therefore all the members were required to sign an engagement to be faithful to the Lord Protector and Commonwealth and to promise not to alter the government as it was settled in a single person and parliament.

About 300 out of the 410 members of parliament duly signed the 'recognition' and resumed their seats; the republicans refused and left the House in order to agitate outside it. Moreover the members who were left, while they voted for the recognition of the Lord Protector and approved in general of his 'fundamentals', did not hesitate to examine, alter and even tear to pieces all except the first clause of the Instrument of Government. Once again the Court proved itself incapable of controlling parliament and finally in desperation Cooper (who was a member of the Council of State), Lambert and one or two others proposed that Cromwell should become King, thus reshaping the government of the country along traditional lines. The proposal was not then considered and Cooper retired in dudgeon from the Council of State. Soon afterwards, on 22 January 1655, its five months being up, Oliver dissolved his first Protectorate Parliament.

In his dissolution speech Oliver spoke more in sorrow than in anger. Since the signature of the recognition, he explained, he had left them alone in the hope that they might have passed 'those good

OLIVER   CROMWELL P.

and wholesome laws which the people had expected from you.' Instead of that he did not know if they had been alive or dead. But what he did know was that they had violated two of his 'fundamentals'. The first was liberty of conscience, the second control of the army. 'Is there not,' he asked, 'yet upon the spirits of men a strange itch? Nothing will satisfy them unless they can put their finger upon their brethren's consciences to pinch them there.' As to the army, they had attempted to undermine his government by failing to provide supplies for its upkeep so that it was 'now upon free quarter'. He concluded his speech by saying: 'I think it my duty to tell you that it is not for the profit of these nations nor fit for the common and public good for you to continue here any longer.'

For the best part of two years that followed, Oliver in effect relied on his old friends in the army – men like Lambert, Fleetwood, Desborough, George Monck and Robert Blake as well as his faithful Secretary of State, John Thurloe – to help him carry on the government. The quarrel between Oliver and his parliament aroused hopes among the Royalists and Levellers alike. A Royalist insurrection, which began in Salisbury in the spring of 1655, was easily crushed, and the new Leveller leader, John Wildman (John Lilburne was wrongfully imprisoned in a lonely castle in Jersey), was put in the Tower of London, later to be released on his promise to become one of Thurloe's spies. To maintain internal security, England and Wales were divided into eleven districts, each under the command of a major-general, who had at his disposal a trained and paid horse militia which he could call upon in an emergency. This scheme had been put forward to the Council of State by a committee of officers and Major-General John Lambert is believed to have been its originator. Oliver Cromwell, it has been said with some justice, never invented anything. But it has been suggested that it was Oliver who added to the major-generals' security duties the task of promoting virtue and suppressing vice. But one must not exaggerate the Puritanism of the major-generals. Some taverns were closed because they were obvious centres of conspiracy; horse-racing was restricted because the crowded courses offered good cover for Royalist meetings. When the Earl of Exeter asked Major-General Whalley if he would allow Lady Grantham's cup to be run for at Lincoln, as he wanted to enter a horse, Whalley replied it was never the intention in suppressing horse races to deprive gentlemen of their sport and he would give permission for the race to be run.

The major-generals were the men whom Oliver trusted most. They included, besides Oliver's cousin Whalley, John Lambert, Charles Fleetwood, Oliver's son-in-law, John Desborough, his brother-in-law, Richard Ingoldsby, Oliver's cousin Goffe (who was Whalley's son-in-law), Berry, who had been captain-lieutenant in Oliver's cavalry regiment, Boteler, who had been a major in Berry's regiment, and Kelsey, who had been a major in Ingoldsby's regiment. So they were a pretty closely knit group. On the other hand, a few of Oliver's officers, among them Harrison and Rich, both Fifth Monarchy men, John Okey, Robert Overton, Edmund Ludlow, Matthew Alured and William Packer, refused to recognize the Protectorate. Robert Blake was to predecease Oliver and John Lambert was to quarrel with him. Thus the army, like parliament, was far from united.

The major-generals took up their duties in the autumn of 1655, six months after the Royalist rising had been put down. At the same time the war against Spain began. Although a 10 per cent tax was imposed on the property of known Royalists to pay for the upkeep of the horse militia, the proceeds did not cover the expense, while the Spanish war magnified the cost of the navy. Thus the major-generals advised Oliver to summon another parliament and ask it for money. They promised that they would ensure that suitable members were elected, but in fact their success was extremely limited. The Council of State took care to see that the members of parliament should recognize the Protectorate before they were allowed into their seats. The new parliament was therefore by no means unfavourably disposed to Cromwell, but many of the members – most of them old hands – were unwilling to accept the constitution of the Protectorate as it stood.

When parliament met in September 1656 Dr John Owen, now Oliver's favourite cleric, preached from the appropriate text: 'What shall one then answer to the Messengers of the Nation? That the Lord had founded Zion, and the Poor of his People shall trust in it?' Oliver followed with a long speech in which he defended the war against Spain – 'The Spaniard,' he said, 'is your enemy naturally by that antipathy that is in him providentially and that in diverse respects.' Then he justified the establishment of the major-generals. Finally he admitted that because taxation had been reduced since the end of the civil wars 'our nation is overwhelmed in debts': so he begged his audience to 'quit themselves like men.' Insofar as the members were asked for money to pay for war, they might have been listening to Charles I or Charles II.

The parliamentarians, like the officers of the army, remained divided in their allegiance to Cromwell. Ninety-nine members were excluded from their seats by the Council of State and another seventy-nine who were allowed in vainly protested against the exclusion of their colleagues. Finally some 160 of the elected members took no part whatever in the immediate proceedings. Those who stayed were in favour of the Spanish war and voted money to pay for it. But the major-generals were universally disliked and a Bill, introduced by Desborough to perpetuate them, was rejected. Oliver blamed the major-generals for having persuaded him to call his second parliament and

Admiral Robert Blake, reputedly a republican but loyal to Oliver Cromwell

thought it served them right that parliament voted them out of existence.

A move began outside parliament for an entirely new constitutional settlement. Let Oliver become king, a constitutional head of state such as John Pym and his friends had wanted Charles I to become in the revolutionary days of the 1640s. The idea was first put forward by Lord Broghill and a group of Anglo-Irish officers and soon they gained the backing of a majority in parliament. They also advocated the restoration of a House of Lords, a Privy Council and a state Church.

When parliament presented Oliver with this draft scheme of government he hesitated for a long time over giving a clear answer to it, as he had hesitated at earlier crises in his political career in 1647, 1648 and 1649 before he sailed to Ireland. He said at his first meeting with parliament to discuss the scheme: 'I should have a very brazen forehead, if it should not beget in me a great deal of consternation of spirit.' It was argued by those who advocated the scheme, such as William Lenthall, formerly Speaker of the House and Master of the Rolls, that the change in Oliver's office was not a mere question of words, a bare title: 'for upon due consideration you shall find that the whole body of the Law is carried upon this wheel, i.e. Kingship.' He was half-persuaded by this line of reasoning. Did not the fundamental laws of the nation define the limits of kingship? If the law knows this 'the people,' he said, 'can know it also, and the people do love what they know.' Not only did Oliver discuss the whole question at length with parliament and committees of parliament, but he held private meetings with his friends like Broghill and Thurloe 'and laying aside his greatness, he would be exceedingly familiar with us [Bulstrode Whitelocke tells the story] and by way of diversion would make verses with us, and everyone must try his fancy ... then he would fall again to his serious and great business and advise with us in those affairs.' But though his civilian advisers like Lenthall, Thurloe, Broghill and Whitelocke urged the change, nearly all his major-generals except Whalley, Goffe and Ingoldsby were adamant republicans; for them the republic was 'the Good Old Cause'; so it was too for most of Oliver's former chaplains such as John Owen, William Dell and Philip Nye. George Fox, the founder of the Society of Friends, sought an interview with Cromwell and begged him only to 'mind the crown that was immortal'.

The leaders of the movement against the Broghill group included John Desborough, Charles Fleetwood, Thomas Pride and John Owen. Several army officers and the London garrison petitioned against Oliver accepting the crown. Finally after three months' discussions he decided to refuse it. Thus he alienated his new friends while his prolonged *hesitations displeased his old ones. But he

A Commonwealth coin (recto and verso) designed by Thomas Simon

Dutch satirical drawing showing Cromwell thinking about becoming king. This is dated 1652 and has nothing to do with the negotiations of 1657 when Cromwell refused the crown

accepted the rest of the proposed constitution with some amendments and on 26 July 1657 the second Protectorate Parliament at last adjourned.

John Lambert, the Yorkshireman who had taken such a big part in drawing up earlier constitutions, refused to take the oath, required as a councillor under the new constitution, to be true to the Lord Protector and to contrive nothing against him. Oliver had no alter- native but to dismiss him. Why Lambert acted in this way is not entirely clear. He was never a fanatical Puritan and seems to have been brought by Fairfax into the war during which he is said to have become 'the darling of the Army', even claiming the credit for Oliver's victories of Preston and Dunbar. At an earlier stage he urged Oliver to become king: under the new constitution the Lord Protector was empowered to nominate his successor. Perhaps John Lambert, who

Oliver Cromwell: the copy of the well-known painting by Robert Walker which was presented to Queen Christina of Sweden (who was later to become a Roman Catholic), the daughter of the Protestant hero, Gustavus Adolphus

was a highly ambitious man, had reason to believe he would not obtain the nomination and might have to fight for the succession. He retired ready to jump forward again when the opportunity arose. He had a beautiful and attractive wife, born Frances Lister (unfortunately no portrait of her survives), who wore dresses sent to her from Paris and whom rumour had it Oliver admired. He may well have stayed with the Lamberts at their Yorkshire home, Calton Hall, and certainly met Frances when she visited her husband during the Scottish campaign of 1651. After Lambert resigned Oliver saw to it that he received a handsome income by way of consolation and Oliver continued to visit the Lamberts at their Surrey home, Wimbledon House. Oliver's favourite daughter, Elizabeth Claypole, is reputed to have disliked Frances Lambert; possibly she was jealous of the attentions her father paid to Frances. But it was all perfectly innocent.

What was the Lord Protector like in private life? How did his greatness become him? In his younger days he had sometimes sported with his soldiers and was not above practical jokes. When he first became a member of parliament, he was said to have the look, though not the bearing, of a country yokel with a reddish complexion and a poorly shaved face. Later his brown hair turned to grey and people noticed a bald spot and the famous warts. Broad-built and about a couple of inches under six feet in height, he seldom lacked dignity. When he became Protector, his Master of Ceremonies hastened to inform Louis XIV of France that if he could not address Oliver as 'brother', the least he expected was 'cousin'.

Oliver was a good family man, but his sons, Richard and Henry, reacted against their father's Puritanism and insisted on marrying wives of their own choice. Oliver's eldest daughter, Bridget, who perhaps took most after him, twice married according to his wishes and so did his daughter Mary. Mrs Cromwell, rather surprised to find herself transmuted into Your Highness, missed the company that she might have enjoyed from a country squire – she once told Oliver 'my life is but half a life in your absence.' She timidly reproached him for not writing more often to his old friends, and when he took her into Whitehall Palace, delighted in ordering copies of his portrait by Walker to present to foreign ambassadors or his fellow rulers. She survived her husband by fourteen years, received an annuity from parliament and died in a country house in Northamptonshire which had belonged to one of her sons-in-law. Oliver's mother was a more formidable figure, a matriarch to whom he was devoted, who died at the age of eighty-nine in the palace of the kings.

Elizabeth Cromwell, a portrait of her when she was Protectress. She is said to have felt uncomfortable in Whitehall

Whitehall Palace from the Thames, showing the Banqueting House in the centre. This palace was used by Cromwell as a home and an office

Dunkirk, the port in the Spanish Netherlands which was handed over to the Cromwellian Protectorate by the French in June 1658

Oliver did not much care for Whitehall and went off punctually most week-ends to Hampton Court where he rode fine horses (in which he took pride), hunted, and in the evenings listened to music played by his organist, John Hingston. He smoked a pipe, was fond of a tankard of ale or a glass of sack (sherry) and preferred good English food, disliking 'foreign kickshaws'. Some of his more Puritan subjects thought that he relaxed his standards after he became Protector and were scandalized when the marriage of his youngest daughter, Frances, was celebrated with mixed dancing and the playing of trumpets and violins. But he was never distracted or corrupted by power.

When parliament met again in January 1658 it had greatly changed in character. A House of Lords had been created to which Oliver had nominated most of his friends and ministers. The members excluded in 1656 were readmitted to the House of Commons. Thus in the Lower House the Court party was weakened and the irreconcilable republicans, again led by Arthur Haselrig and Thomas Scot, strengthened. In his first speech to parliament, Oliver assured the members that they now enjoyed the blessings of peace and a godly

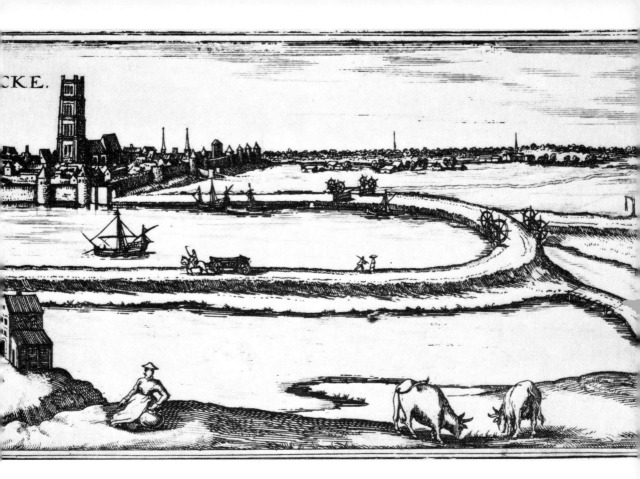

ministry. In a second speech Oliver spoke to them of foreign affairs and public finance. He warned them of unrest in Scotland, advised them on the continuing war against Spain, and stressed the need to help keep the peace between the Protestant kings in the Baltic. He emphasized the importance of having an army which could fight upon the continental mainland: 'You have accounted yourselves happy in being environed with a great ditch from all the world beside. Truly you will not be able to keep your ditch nor your shipping unless you turn your ships and your shipping into troops of horse and companies of foot and fight to defend yourselves on *terra firma.*'

In fact the foreign policy of the Lord Protector was remarkably successful in spite of some setbacks. Robert Blake inflicted a severe defeat on the Spanish galleons anchored off the Canary Islands, and earlier a Spanish treasure fleet was captured. An offensive alliance with France against Spain, which Oliver signed in March 1657, promised that if England provided an expeditionary force in Spanish Flanders, supported by a fleet, she would be rewarded with possession of the port of Dunkirk. English redcoats took an important part in the battle of the Dunes, fought in June 1658, and the French reluctantly

By the Protector.

A PROCLAMATION

Giving Encouragement to such as shall transplant themselves to *Jamaica*.

Whereas the Island of Jamaica in America, is by the Providence of God, in the hands and possession of this State, the Enemy which was found upon it, being fled into the Mountains with an intention to escape into other places, save such of them as do daily render themselves to our Commander in chief there, to be disposed of by him; and we being satisfied of the Goodness, Fertility, and Commodiousness for Trade and Commerce of that Island, Have resolved, by the blessing of God, to use Our best endeavours to secure, and plant the same. For which end and purpose, we have thought it necessary to publish, and make known unto the People of this Commonwealth, and especially to those of the English Islands, Plantations and Colonies in America, our Resolutions and Intentions on that behalf, as also to declare unto them the Encouragements which we have thought fit to give unto such as shall remove themselves, and their habitations into the aforesaid Island of Jamaica, within the time mentioned and expressed in these Presents. And first, concerning the securing thereof against the Enemy, We have already upon the Island, which landed there in May last, above six thousand Souldiers, and the beginning of July after, we sent from hence a Regiment of eight hundred more, drawn out of Our old Regiments in England, with eight Ships of War, besides Victualers, to be added to twelve others, that were left there by General Pen, under the command of Captain Will. Goodson, all which are appointed to remain in those Seas for the Defence of the said Island; and we shall from time to time take care to send thither other, both Land and Sea Forces, that we may have alwaies in those parts, such a strength as may be able, through the blessing of God, to defend and secure it against any Attempt of the Enemy; that whereas the Planters in other Places have been at Great and vast expences at their first sitting down, and in the very beginning of their Plantations for their necessary defence, aswell against the Natives of the Countrey as other Enemies, those who shall remove thither, will be under the immediate Protection of this State, and so eased both of the danger and charge which other Plantations are subject to, and shall have, for their further encouragement, the terms and conditions following.

1. Those who shall transport themselves as aforesaid shall have land set forth unto them, according to the proportion of twenty Acres, besides Lakes and Rivers, for every Male of twelve years old and upwards, and ten Acres for every other Male or Female, in some convenient place of the said Island; and in case any whole Plantation, That is to say, the Governours and greatest part of the people shall remove themselves, they shall be preferred in respect of the place of their sitting down, that it may be near some good Harbour commodious for Commerce and Navigation.

2. That the said Proportion of Land shall be set forth unto them, within six weeks after notice given by them under their hands, or the hands of some of them on the behalf of the rest, unto his Highness Commander in chief, or Commissioners there, appointed for that purpose of their resolutions to remove, and of the time they intend to be upon the place.

Proclamation by the Lord Protector giving encouragement to those willing to become colonists in Jamaica, which was captured by Cromwell's forces in 1655

handed over Dunkirk. The capture of the island of Jamaica in the Spanish West Indies during 1655, though considered a disappointment at the time, was to be the foundation of a prosperous part of the British Empire in the eighteenth century. The English navy, over 150 warships strong, was able to enforce the Navigation Act of 1651 against the Dutch, at any rate in European waters outside the Baltic, and thus broke the Dutch monopoly in the carrying trade. In February 1658 English ambassadors sent out by Cromwell were able to mediate peace for a time between Sweden and Denmark. Oliver realized that it was vital to the interests of England to keep the peace in the Baltic because nearly all her naval supplies came from there and in exchange woollen cloth, stockings and leather goods were exported. A recent expert re-examination of Cromwell's policy in the Baltic contends that it was 'sound in its objectives, appropriate in its choice of means and (by and large) correctly calculated.' (Michael Roberts.) If Oliver sometimes dreamed of a European Protestant union, he also envisaged obtaining Bremen and Gibraltar as well as Dunkirk and Jamaica as outposts of a British imperial Commonwealth. When he died, he left England beyond doubt a great power.

But Cromwell's last parliament was little interested in foreign affairs or national greatness. The republican leaders, agitating and filibustering, were determined to destroy the new constitution, to over-throw the new House of Lords, to undermine the Protector and, if possible, to secure the recall of the Rump Parliament, whose limited virtues they painted in streaks of gold. Oliver was never a patient man and he watched the proceedings of the House of Commons with growing irritation. He perceived the dangers of an alliance between republicans, extreme sectaries and part of the army, which had been foreshadowed by his former friend, Harry Vane, in his pamphlet *A Healing Question Propounded and Resolved*, published in 1656; and he was alarmed over a petition concocted in London on behalf of 'the Good Old Cause' which was to be presented to parliament. He believed such dissensions could have no end but anarchy.

On 4 February 1658, an icy day, Oliver ate an early dinner, then seized hold of the nearest available coach and drove to Westminster, determined to dissolve parliament. He had not consulted his Privy Council and when Charles Fleetwood (who had taken Lambert's place as Oliver's second in command) attempted to dissuade him, he retorted: 'You are a milksop, by the living God I will dissolve this parliament.' He spoke extemporaneously to the members present in

A map of Jamaica and the title-page of *Jamaica Viewed*, published in 1661 to promote settlement in the former Spanish island

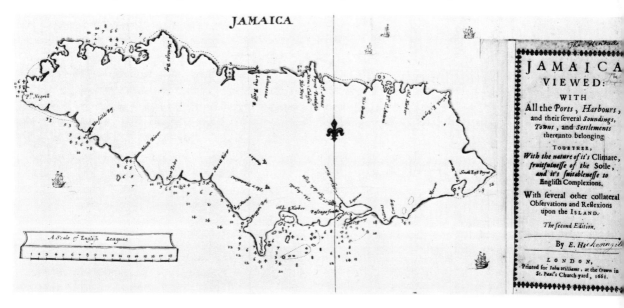

107

grief and reproach, warning them that Charles II stood ready to invade and that the nation might be plunged once more into blood and confusion. In conclusion he said: 'I think it is high time that an end be put to your sitting and I do declare to you here that I do dissolve this parliament. Let God judge between you and me.' 'Amen,' answered the defiant republicans.

Two days later Oliver invited the principal officers of the army to a great feast in the Cockpit opposite his palace. He tried to create a friendly atmosphere by saying that he would not be 'like the parson who preached for an hour to whom nobody was allowed to reply.' Then he defended the dissolution of parliament as necessary for public safety and claimed that the army and the City of London were being tampered with. The wine flowed freely and in a glow of euphoria the officers promised to 'stand and fall, live and die with my Lord Protector.'

But the unity of the army was somewhat superficial and later that February the Lord Protector interviewed several officers individually. He was irate about the attitude of William Packer, the acting colonel of his own cavalry regiment, who had risen from the ranks, having enlisted as a young man in Oliver's first troop of horse and served him loyally for fourteen years. Packer was particularly annoyed by the establishment of a new House of Lords and echoed Vane in accusing Oliver of betraying 'the Good Old Cause'. When Oliver asked him what the Good Old Cause was, he took refuge in generalities. Oliver felt compelled to dismiss Packer with five other officers in his regiment and other changes had to be made in the composition of the army. But if dissatisfaction existed in the army in England, Oliver could still rely upon the armies in Ireland and Scotland. His son Henry, now Commander-in-Chief in Ireland, assured his father that the army was loyal almost to a man. Monck's devotion to Oliver was never shaken; he ruled Scotland with an iron hand.

Unquestionably Oliver's physical and mental strength declined rapidly during the last years of his life. The doctors had no cure or even palliative for the malaria that he had picked up in the Irish bogs. He was periodically ill, for example both after his speech to the officers, when he took to his bed, and during the prolonged discussions on kingship. In April 1658 Henry Cromwell wrote about his father to their mutual friend Lord Broghill: 'I wish he was equally distant from both his childhoods.' Later his son questioned whether domestic peace did not depend upon his father's life, skill and personal interest in the army. Thurloe feared that the Lord Protector was losing his gift for leadership. Oliver was certainly worried sick over the possibility of another Royalist rising and an invasion from abroad; he had reason to fear it since in 1656 Charles II had concluded two treaties with the King of Spain and now that the seemingly interminable

Two examples of Oliver
Cromwell's signature dated 1651
(*right*) and 1657 (*below*). The
second signature is to a letter
dismissing Major-General John
Lambert

war between Spain and France was tottering to its end, the exiled English King hoped to invade with the aid of a Spanish army.

David Lloyd George was fond of quoting a saying by Lord Rendel: 'there are no friends at the top.' Though Oliver could count on his son Henry and on George Monck, in London he really had only Thurloe, who had more of the character of a permanent civil servant than of an astute and inventive statesman, as Lambert and the dead Ireton had been. Charles Fleetwood, who since Lambert's dismissal looked after the army in England, was a weak man, incapable of making up his mind about anything. Colonel John Desborough, Colonel Edward Whalley and Colonel William Goffe, who were all active members of the Privy Council, had been estranged by Cromwell's abandonment of the major-generals and by his toying with the idea of kingship. Thomas Harrison, who refused to pledge himself not to disturb the public peace, was imprisoned in Carisbrooke Castle. Major-General Edmund Ludlow, once acting Commander-in-Chief in Ireland, had to be placed under strict surveillance after he had given his parole. Harry Vane, who accused Oliver to his face of betraying the cause of truth and righteousness, was also to languish in Carisbrooke. Even Oliver's friends, the former army chaplains, headed by John Owen, disliked the royal aspects of the new Protectorate, while officers who had served him loyally in the heady days of the civil wars came to believe more and more in the imminent return of Christ to earth and thought that Oliver had no right to usurp His throne.

During the six months following the dissolution of parliament Oliver was chiefly concerned with foreign policy. On 10 July 1658 he left Whitehall for Hampton Court where he presided over meetings of his Privy Council. There he kept watch over his favourite daughter, Elizabeth Claypole, who tried vainly to conceal her cancer from him; and he himself took waters from Tunbridge Wells to maintain his health, and opium to assure him sleep. One who knew him well was to write of 'the sympathy of his spirit with his sorely afflicted daughter' which came on top of the burdens of government and the censures of his former friends. Elizabeth died in agony on 10 August but Oliver himself was too sick to attend her funeral when her coffin was taken down the river in a flotilla to Westminster Abbey. Sometime during that August, possibly on the 17th, George Fox, the Quaker leader, met Oliver in Hampton Court park and afterwards recorded that he 'felt a waft of death go forth against him' and that 'he looked like a dead man.' On 24 August, on the advice of his doctors, Oliver returned to Whitehall while St James's Palace (believed to be healthier than either Hampton Court or Whitehall because it was further from the stench of the Thames) was prepared for him. But by the beginning of the following week he was so crippled by attacks of malaria that prayers were said on the Sabbath throughout the land for his recovery.

Elizabeth Claypole, reputedly Oliver's favourite daughter, who died of cancer in 1658, predeceasing her father

On Monday 30 August a terrible storm began which lasted intermittently until the Friday. During that week Oliver knew that he was dying. He put his faith in the covenant of Grace with the Almighty. He said: 'It is not my design to drink or to sleep, but ... to make what haste I can to be gone.' He believed that God had made him 'a mean instrument' to do His people 'some good' and Himself service. He expired at three o'clock in the afternoon of 3 September, the anniversary of his victories at Dunbar and Worcester. An autopsy was conducted that evening and on the next day his body was embalmed. On 20 September the embalmed body was taken by night from Whitehall to Somerset House. Here during a ceremonial lying-in-state the general public were invited to pay their last respects to the dead ruler. In the early morning of 10 November the body was removed from Somerset House and secretly interred in the Henry VII chapel at Westminster Abbey. On 23 November an elaborate State funeral, costing tens of thousands of pounds, commemorated with mourning the death of Oliver.

A contemporary engraving showing Oliver Cromwell's lying-in-state in Somerset House

After the Restoration of Charles II in May 1660 the bodies of all the Commonwealth heroes were dug out of their tombs in the Abbey and cast into a pit, all that is except the body of John Pym, the leader of the parliamentary revolution, which must have been mislaid, and that of Edward Popham, one of Cromwell's generals-at-sea whose relatives were influential Royalists. The remains of Oliver's old mother and daughter were among those desecrated. On 30 January 1661 Oliver's own body was carried to Tyburn, where criminals were executed, and hung up in green waxed cloth from morning until dusk. Then the embalmed head was severed from the body and placed on a pole on top of Westminster Hall where it remained throughout the whole of Charles II's reign. The body was buried beneath Tyburn gallows.

(*Below*) imaginative Dutch print showing the preparations being made for the hanging of Cromwell's disinterred body at Tyburn in 1661

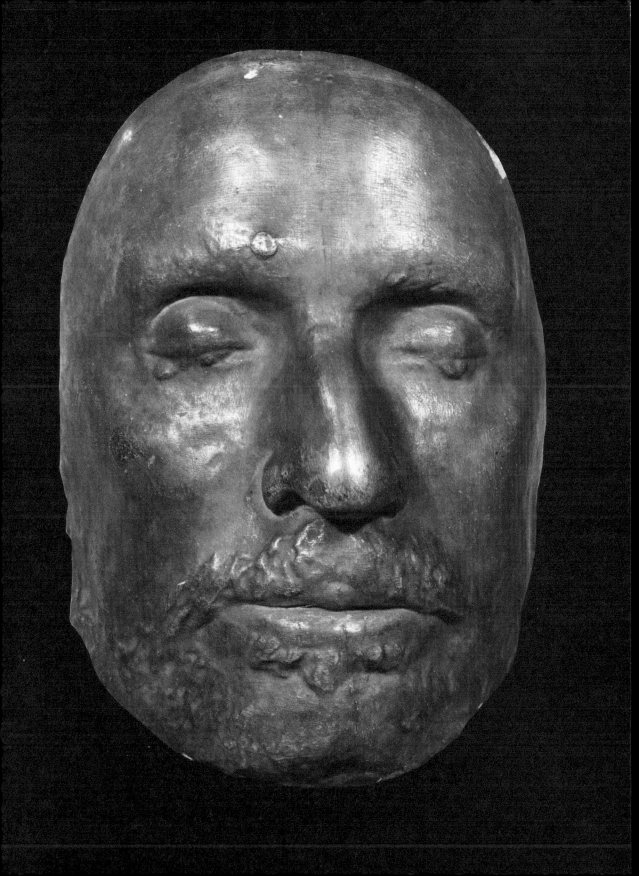

What had Oliver Cromwell achieved? He had established the British Commonwealth as a great power in Europe; he had preached and practised 'liberty of conscience' not only for all kinds of Christians but also for Jews, to whom, against fierce opposition even from his own Council, he allowed their own synagogue and cemetery in London; lastly he raised the stature of parliament which, in spite of his own difficulties with it, was never again to be completely thrust aside, as Charles I had thrust it aside for eleven years. Charles II followed in Cromwell's footsteps by trying to secure liberty of conscience for all his Christian subjects; by claiming (with his tongue in his cheek) that he 'loved parliaments'; by trying to maintain an independent foreign policy, though, after being twice defeated by the Dutch, he ended more or less as a vassal of France. No one considered that England (the union with Scotland and Ireland had been dissolved) was any longer a great power; and many ordinary Englishmen sighed for the wonderful days of Oliver. Even Charles II's Lord Chancellor, the Earl of Clarendon, was to write that 'Cromwell's greatness at home was but a shadow of the glory he had abroad.'

The last year of Oliver's life was the saddest. Of course the Levellers and the strict republicans never forgave him when he assumed the title of Lord Protector. But most of his officers and chaplains understood that what he aimed at was a balanced government with nothing arbitrary about it. In fact Oliver was never a dictator in the modern sense of the term. Yet when he seriously contemplated becoming a king, taking three months to make up his mind before he refused that title, his world began to disintegrate and those who had fought the long fight with him against what they considered was the tyranny of Charles I felt that, urged on by new and evil friends, he was betraying the Good Old Cause. In the end he revealed the sentiments of a dynast when he chose his inexperienced and incompetent eldest son, Richard, to be his successor. Then only three friends outside his immediate family circle remained loyal to his memory: the dour George Monck, the devoted John Thurloe, and the faithful Hugh Peter, whom Oliver had employed as a Jack of all trades until the last.

On the Sunday after his master died Hugh Peter preached a sermon in Whitehall in his capacity of chaplain to the Privy Council. He took as his text: 'Moses my servant is dead; now therefore arise, go over this Jordan, thou and all this people, unto the land which I do give to them, even to the children of Israel.' But the people who had followed Oliver Cromwell to Mount Sinai never reached their promised land.

CHRONOLOGY

1599 25 April. Oliver Cromwell is born in Huntingdon.

1616 23 April. Oliver becomes fellow-commoner of Sidney Sussex College, Cambridge.

1617 June. Oliver's father dies; he leaves Cambridge and returns home.

1620 22 August. Oliver Cromwell marries Elizabeth Bourchier at St Giles church, Cripplegate.

1628 17 March. Oliver enters House of Commons as member of parliament for Huntingdon.

1629 11 February. Oliver attacks bishops in speech in House of Commons.

1640 25 March. Oliver is elected member of parliament for Cambridge and attends meeting of Short Parliament.
3 November. The Long Parliament meets.

1642 22 August. The civil war begins. Oliver raises a troop of cavalry at Huntingdon.

1643 January. Oliver becomes a colonel and begins forming a double regiment of cavalry.
11 October. Battle of Winceby.

1644 22 January. Oliver Cromwell is appointed lieutenant-general in the army of the Eastern Association commanded by the Earl of Manchester.

2 July. Lieutenant-General Cromwell takes charge of left wing of Parliamentarian army at battle of Marston Moor.
9 December. Oliver supports Self-Denying Ordinance in House of Commons.

1645 10 June. Oliver is appointed lieutenant-general in New Model Army commanded by Sir Thomas Fairfax and takes part in battle of Naseby on 14 June.

1647 3 June. Oliver, after vainly trying to reconcile the King, the parliament and the army, throws in his lot with the army and on 28 October takes chair at meeting of the General Council of the Army at Putney.

1648 3 May. Lieutenant-General Cromwell leaves London in command of army which besieges Pembroke and then marches north to win battle of Preston on 17 August. He then visits Scotland and returns to take part in siege of Pontefract.
6 December. Oliver arrives back in London after Colonel Pride's Purge of the House of Commons.
26 December. Oliver decides to push through trial of Charles I.

1649 30 January. Execution of Charles I.
14 February. Oliver Cromwell becomes member of Council of State of the Commonwealth which replaces the monarchy.
13 August. Oliver sails to Ireland in command of expeditionary force.

1650 26 May. Oliver returns to London from Ireland.
26 June. Oliver Cromwell is appointed Captain-General of Commonwealth and leads army to Scotland.
3 September. Battle of Dunbar.

1651 3 September. Battle of Worcester.

1653 20 April. Oliver dissolves the Rump Parliament.
4 July. Oliver addresses Assembly of Saints picked by the army.
12 December. Oliver Cromwell becomes Lord Protector of the Commonwealth under the Instrument of Government.

1654 3 September. Oliver addresses first Protectorate Parliament.
26 December. Oliver dispatches amphibious force to Spanish West Indies where it seizes Jamaica.

1655 22 January. First Protectorate Parliament is dissolved.
28 May. Beginnings of system of dividing England into groups of counties under command of major-generals of horse militia to reinforce local government.
24 October. General war begins against Spain.

1656 17 September. Oliver opens second Protectorate Parliament.

1657 29 January. System of major-generals is ended.

23 March. Anglo-French offensive alliance against Spain is signed.

31 March. 'Humble Petition and Advice' containing monarchical scheme of government is submitted by parliament to Lord Protector.

8 May. Oliver refuses offer of crown by parliament.

1658 4 February. Oliver Cromwell dissolves second Protectorate Parliament.

4 June. British troops serving under Marshal Turenne take part in battle of the Dunes against Spanish army. Dunkirk is handed over by French to Cromwell's government.

3 September. Death of Cromwell in Whitehall palace.

23 November. State funeral of the Lord Protector Oliver Cromwell.

1661 30 January. Oliver Cromwell's remains, disinterred from Westminster Abbey, are buried beneath the gallows at Tyburn.

BIBLIOGRAPHY

The best and fairest biography remains, more than seventy years after its first publication, that by the late Sir Charles Firth. W.C. Abbott's edition of *The Writings and Speeches of Oliver Cromwell* (1937–47) is the most recent and fullest, although neither the editing nor the linking narrative is beyond criticism.

Since my own book, *The Greatness of Oliver Cromwell*, appeared in 1957 (a corrected edition was published by Collier Books as a paperback in 1962 and 1966) several important articles and books touching on various aspects of Cromwell and his world have become available. I have made use of them – and one or two other books which I missed at the time – in the present book. They are as follows:

BOOKS

Peter Barraclough *John Owen* 1961
J.H. Hexter *The Reign of King Pym* 1960
Gertrude Huehns *Antinomianism in English History* 1951
G.F. Nuttall *The Holy Spirit in Puritan Faith and Experience* 1946
Leo F. Solt *Saints in Arms* 1959
R.P. Stearns *The Strenuous Puritan: Hugh Peter, 1558–1660* 1954
Eric C. Walker *William Dell* 1971
C.V. Wedgwood *The King's War 1641–1647* 1958
C.V. Wedgwood *The Trial of Charles I* 1964
David Underdown *Pride's Purge* 1971
George Yule *The Independents in the English Civil War* 1958

ARTICLES

G.E. Aylmer 'Was Oliver Cromwell a Member of the Army in 1646–7 or not?' *History* 1971
George D. Heath III 'Cromwell and Lambert 1653–1657': *The Historian* 1959
Valerie Pearl 'Oliver St John and the "Middle Group" in the Long Parliament': *English Historical Review* 1966
Michael Roberts 'Cromwell and the Baltic': *Essays in Swedish History* 1967
H.R. Trevor-Roper 'The Fast Sermons of the Long Parliament', 'Oliver Cromwell and his Parliaments' and 'Scotland in the Puritan Revolution': *Religion, the Reformation and Social Change* 1967
David Underdown 'The Parliamentary Diary of John Boys': *Bulletin of the Institute of Historical Research* 1966
'Cromwell and the Officers 1658': *English Historical Review* 1968
A.H. Woolrych 'The Good Old Cause and the Fall of the Protectorate': *Cambridge Historical Journal* 1957
'The Calling of Barebone's Parliament': *English Historical Review* 1965
Blair Worden 'The Bill for a New Representative: the dissolution of the Long Parliament April 1653': *English Historical Review* 1971

LIST OF ILLUSTRATIONS

buted to Robert Walker (1607–58 or 1660). National Portrait Gallery, London

16 Execution of Thomas Wentworth, first Earl of Strafford, 1641; contempory engraving by Wenceslaus Hollar. British Museum, Department of Prints and Drawings

17 Lower House of Parliament; engraving, c. 1640. British Museum, Department of Prints and Drawings

18 King Charles I's order for the arrest of five members of parliament, 1641; manuscript. British Museum. MS Eg. 2546, f. 20. Photo Mansell Collection

Title-page of *An Exact and true Relation of the late Plots which were contrived and hatched in Ireland*, 1641. British Museum, Department of Printed Books

19 Map of Ireland 'with particular notes distinguishing the townes revolted, taken or burnt since the late Rebellion'; engraved broadsheet, c. 1642. British Museum, Department of Printed Books

20 King Charles I with Sir Edward Walker, reputedly in the grounds of Nottingham Castle; painting by an unknown artist, 17th century. National Portrait Gallery, London

21 Oliver Cromwell; painting by Robert Walker, c. 1649. National Portrait Gallery, London

22 Map of England at the time of the Civil War

23 Nottingham; engraving after Richard Hall from Robert Thoroton: *Antiquities of Nottinghamshire*, 1677. British Museum, Department of Printed Books

23 A crown minted during the siege of Oxford, c. 1646. British Museum, Department of Coins and Medals. Photo Ray Gardner

24 The Solemn League and Covenant, 1643; contemporary engraving by Wenceslaus Hollar. British Museum, Department of Prints and Drawings

25 Queen Henrietta Maria; painting by Anthony van Dyck, c. 1639. By gracious permission of Her Majesty the Queen

26 Prince Rupert; woodcut frontispiece to *The Bloody Prince or the Most Cruell Practices of Prince Rupert*, 1643. British Museum, Department of Printed Books

Cavalry tactics; engravings from John Cruso: *Militarie Instructions for the Cavallrie*, 1632. British Museum, Department of Printed Books

27 Prince Rupert; painting by the studio of Anthony van Dyck, c. 1637. National Portrait Gallery, London

28 Cavaliers; woodcuts from the title-page of *The Exercise of the English in the Militia of the Kingdome of England*, early 17th century. Mansell Collection

29 Edward Montagu, second Earl of Manchester; painting by Peter Lely, c. 1661–65. National Portrait Gallery, London

30 Puritan troopers pillaging churches on the way to York; engraving by Wenceslaus Hollar from John Vicars: *Sight of the Transactions of These Latter Yeares*, 1646. Mansell Collection

Sir James Lumsden's plan of the

battle of Marston Moor, 1644; manuscript with Brigadier Peter Young's extrapolations. Reproduced from Peter Young: *Marston Moor, 1644. The Campaign and the Battle* by kind permission of the author and the publishers, The Roundwood Press Ltd

32 York; engraving, 1678. British Museum, Map Room

Alexander Leslie, first Earl of Leven; painting, 17th century. Scottish National Portrait Gallery, Edinburgh. Photo National Galleries of Scotland

33 A ninepenny piece, cast at Newark, 1645. British Museum, Department of Coins and Medals. Photo Ray Gardner

35 Satirical medal of Thomas Fairfax as a Jester, 1650. British Museum, Department of Coins and Medals. Photo Ray Gardner

Thomas Fairfax; painting attributed to Edward Bower (1612–71). By courtesy of the Earl Spencer. Photo Henry Cooper and Son

36 Uniform of a trooper of the New Model Army. Tower of London Armouries. Photo Department of the Environment

Soldier carved on the staircase of Cromwell House, Highgate, *c.* 1638. Montford Missionary Society. Photo Eileen Tweedy

Priming flask with the initials 'O.C.' thought to have belonged to Oliver Cromwell. Cromwell Museum, Huntingdon. Photo Eileen Tweedy

Devices used by Parliament Officers during the civil wars; engraving, 18th century. British Museum, Department of Prints and Drawings

37 Cavaliers at the siege of Chester; engraving after the very Reverend Hugh Cholmondeley of the 17th-century window in Farndon Church, Cheshire. Grosvenor Museum, Chester

38 Plan of Oxford, 1644; manuscript. Bodleian Library, Oxford. MS Wood 376B, f. 30

40 Battle of Naseby; engraving from Joshua Sprigge: *Anglia Rediviva*, 1647. British Museum, Department of Printed Books

42 Hugh Peter; detail of a painting by William Dobson (1610–46). Courtesy of Lord Tollemache. Photo Courtauld Institute of Art, London

William Dell; painting, 17th century. Gonville and Caius College, Cambridge. Photo W. Eaden Lilley and Co. Ltd

43 Title-page of *The Souldiers Catechisme*, 1644. On loan to Cromwell Museum, Huntingdon. Trustees of the London Museum. Photo Eileen Tweedy

Opening page of *The New Common Prayer Book*, 1644. Cromwell Museum, Huntingdon. Photo Eileen Tweedy

44 Oliver Cromwell's house, Clerkenwell Close, London; engraving, 18th century. Mansell Collection

45 Richard Cromwell; painting attributed to Robert Walker (1607–58 or 1660). Cromwell Museum, Huntingdon. Photo Eileen Tweedy

Mary Cromwell; painting, 17th

century. Cromwell Museum, Huntingdon. Photo Eileen Tweedy

45 Frances Cromwell; painting attributed to John Riley (1646–91). Cromwell Museum, Huntingdon. Photo Eileen Tweedy

Bridget Cromwell; facsimile of painting by Peter Lely (1618–80). Cromwell Museum, Huntingdon. Photo Eileen Tweedy

47 *England's Miraculous Preservation Emblematically Described*; engraving from a broadsheet, 1646. British Museum, Department of Prints and Drawings

Thomas Fairfax presiding over the Council of the Army, 1647; contemporary woodcut

48 Henry Ireton; painting attributed to Robert Walker, *c.* 1650–60. National Portrait Gallery, London

49 The Sun Inn, Saffron Walden. Photo British Tourist Authority

51 Interior of Saffron Walden Church. Photo Royal Commission on Historical Monuments

52 John Lambert; painting after Robert Walker, *c.* 1650–55. National Portrait Gallery, London

Hampton Court Palace; painting, *c.* 1640. By gracious permission of Her Majesty the Queen

56 Woodcut title-page from *His Majesties Demands to Collonel Hammond*, 1648. British Museum, Department of Printed Books

57 Carisbrooke Castle; pen and wash drawing by J. Hadley, 1756. Victoria and Albert Museum, London, Print Room. Photo John Webb

57 Carisbrooke Castle. Photo Aerofilms

58 Pembroke Castle. Photo British Tourist Authority

59 Pembroke Castle; pen and wash drawing by Francis Place, *c.* 1699. Victoria and Albert Museum, London, Print Room. Photo John Webb

60 King Charles I with the parliamentary commissioners; woodcut title-page from *A Declaration for Peace from the Kings Most Excellent Majesty*, 1648. British Museum, Department of Printed Books

61 King Charles I; detail from the triple portrait by Anthony van Dyck, 1635. By gracious permission of Her Majesty the Queen

62 Warrant for the execution of King Charles I, dated 1648; manuscript (facsimile). Mansell Collection

63 Trial of King Charles I, 1649; contemporary engraving. Mansell Collection

64 Execution of King Charles I; engraving, 18th century

65 Oliver Cromwell; marble bust by Edward Pierce, *c.* 1654–58 or posthumous. Ashmolean Museum, Oxford, Department of Western Art

66 Equestrian portrait of Oliver Cromwell; engraving by François Mazot, mid 17th century. National Portrait Gallery, London

68 Title-page of John Lilburne: *An Impeachment of High Treason against Oliver Cromwell*, 1649. British Museum, Department of Prints and Drawings

69 John Lilburne whipped at the cart's tail, 1645; engraving from a contemporary Dutch broadsheet. British Museum, Department of Prints and Drawings.

John Lilburne; engraving by George Glover from Richard Overton: *A Remonstrance of Many Learned Citizens*, 1646. British Museum. Department of Prints and Drawings

71 Dr John Owen; engraving by George Vertue (1684–1756). Victoria and Albert Museum, London, Print Room. Photo John Webb

George Monck; engraving attributed to Robert Gaywood (*c.* 1650-*c.*1711). Victoria and Albert Museum, London, Print Room

72 Drogheda; pen and wash drawing, *c.* 1680. British Museum, Department of Prints and Drawings. Mansell Collection

Map of the Irish campaign, 1649–50

75 The Scots holding King Charles II's nose to the grindstone; engraving from *Old Sayings and Predictions Verified and Fulfilled Touching the Young King of Scotland and His Gued Subjects*, 1651. British Museum, Department of Prints and Drawings

76 Battle of Dunbar; engraving by Peter Stent for Payne Fisher, 1650. Ashmolean Museum, Oxford, Department of Western Art

77 Medal commemorating the battle of Dunbar, 1651. British Museum, Department of Coins and Medals. Photo Ray Gardner

Woodcut from a broadsheet, *Jockies Lamentation*; 1650. British Museum, Department of Printed Books

78 Stirling; painting attributed to Jan Vosterman, *c.* 1673–74. Smith Institute, Stirling. Photo National Monuments Record of Scotland

79 Edinburgh; engraving by Georg Braun and Frans Hogenberg from *Civitates Orbis Terrarum*, 1660. British Museum, Map Room

80 Plan of Worcester, 1651; engraving, 1662. British Museum, Map Room

83 The House of Commons, 1651; verso of the Great Seal of England. British Museum, Department of Manuscripts. Attached to MS Sloane 3243, dated 8 September 1656

84 Oliver Cromwell dismissing the Rump Parliament, 1653; contemporary Dutch engraving. British Museum, Department of Prints and Drawings

86 Battle of Leghorn, 12 March 1653; painting by Reinier Nooms (*c.* 1623–before 1668). Rijksmuseum, Amsterdam

87 Oliver Cromwell rejecting Holland's offer of peace, 1653; engraving from a contemporary Dutch broadsheet. British Museum, Department of Prints and Drawings

88 Oliver Cromwell's seal. The Cromwell Museum, Huntingdon. Photo Eileen Tweedy

Impression of the seal of the Protectorate, 1655. Cromwell Museum, Huntingdon. Photo Eileen Tweedy

Oliver Cromwell's Sword of

State. Cromwell Museum, Huntingdon. Photo Eileen Tweedy

Proclamation declaring Oliver Cromwell Lord Protector, December 1653. Guildhall Library, London

89 *The Embleme of Englands Distractions*; engraving by William Faithorne, 1658. Mansell Collection

90 Anthony Ashley Cooper; engraving by Jacobus Houbraken after Peter Lely, *c*. 1647. Victoria and Albert Museum, London, Print Room. Photo John Webb

John Milton; engraving by William Faithorne, 1670. British Museum, Department of Printed Books

91 John Thurloe; painting by William Dobson (1610-46). Courtesy of the Chequers Trust

92 Title-page from an *Ordinance Prohibiting Cock-Matches*, 1654. Cromwell Museum, Huntingdon. Photo Eileen Tweedy

Engraved title-page from *Catch That Catch Can, or a Choice Collection of Catches, Rounds & Canons*, 1652. British Museum, Department of Printed Books

A company of Puritans; painting attributed to Caspar Netscher, mid or later 17th century. Courtesy J. O. Flatter Esq.

94 Charles Fleetwood; miniature by John Hoskins, 17th century. Courtesy of the Earl of Beauchamp. Photo Baylis

Henry Cromwell (?); miniature by Samuel Cooper (1609-72). The Duke of Buccleuch and Queensbery, K.T., G.C.V.O. Photo Victoria and Albert Museum, London

95 Medal commemorating the end of the Anglo-Dutch war, 1654. British Museum, Department of Coins and Medals. Photo Ray Gardner

97 Oliver Cromwell; painting by Peter Lely, *c*. 1654. City Museum and Art Gallery, Birmingham

99 Admiral Robert Blake; miniature attributed to Samuel Cooper (1609-72). National Maritime Museum, Greenwich

100 Commonwealth crown designed by Thomas Simon, 1656-58. British Museum, Department of Coins and Medals. Photo Ray Gardner

101 Satire on Oliver Cromwell considering kingship; engraving from a Dutch broadsheet, 1652. British Museum, Department of Prints and Drawings

102 Oliver Cromwell; painting attributed to Robert Walker (1607-58 or 1660). Nationalmuseum, Stockholm. Photo Svenska Porträttarkivet, Stockholm

103 Elizabeth Cromwell, Oliver Cromwell's wife; painting attributed to Peter Lely (1618-80). Cromwell Museum, Huntingdon. Photo Eileen Tweedy

Whitehall from the Thames; engraving by Wenceslaus Hollar (1607-77). Guildhall Library, London

104 Dunkirk; engraving, 1650. British Museum, Map Room

106 *Proclamation Giving Encouragement to*

Such as Shall Transplant Themselves to Jamaica, 1655. Guildhall Library, London

107 Frontispiece map and title-page of E. Hickeringill: *Jamaica Viewed*, 1661. British Museum, Department of Printed Books

109 Pass for Mrs Ann Bruce and others 'to pass on to Kerney and receive their goods there'; manuscript signed by Oliver Cromwell, 20 August 1651. The Pierpont Morgan Library, New York

Letter to Major-General John Lambert demanding the surrender of his Commission; manuscript signed by Oliver Cromwell, 13 July 1657. Cromwell Museum, Huntingdon. Photo Eileen Tweedy

110 Elizabeth Cromwell, Oliver Cromwell's daughter; painting, 17th century. Cromwell Museum, Huntingdon. Photo Eileen Tweedy

111 Oliver Cromwell's lying-in-state, 1658; engraving, 1659. British Museum, Department of Prints and Drawings

112 Exhumation of the Regicides; engraving from a Dutch broadsheet, 1660. British Museum, Department of Prints and Drawings

113 Death mask of Oliver Cromwell, 1658. National Portrait Gallery, London

115 Statue of Oliver Cromwell by William Hamo Thorneycroft, 1899, London. Photo British Tourist Authority

INDEX

References in italics refer to illustrations